NEW YORK

BEAUTY · DIVERSIFIED

Linda J. Hahn

AQS Publishing

JUN 2013

Located in Paducah, Kentucky, the American Quilter's Society (AQS) is dedicated to promoting the accomplishments of today's quilters. Through its publications and events, AQS strives to honor today's quiltmakers and their work and to inspire future creativity and innovation in quiltmaking.

Executive Book Editor: Andi Milam Reynolds
Graphic Design: Lynda Smith
Cover Design: Michael Buckingham
Quilt Photography: Charles R. Lynch

Additional copies of this book may be ordered from the American Quilter's Society, PO Box 3290, Paducah, KY 42002-3290, or online at www.AmericanQuilter.com.

Text © 2013, Author, Linda J. Hahn
Artwork © 2013, American Quilter's Society

Library of Congress Cataloging-in-Publication Data

Hahn, Linda.
  New York Beauty Diversified / By Linda J. Hahn.
     pages cm
  Summary: "The paper-piecing technique for the precise block that Linda Hahn showed in her first book, New York Beauty Simplified, is joined with 8 traditional quilt blocks to bring fresh life to this old beauty. 19 projects showcase the numerous design possibilities for everyone from beginning quilters to experienced sewers. Quilting patterns for each project are included"--Provided by publisher.
  ISBN 978-1-60460-058-2
  1. Patchwork--Patterns. 2. New York beauty quilts. I. Title.
TT835.H257 2013
746.46--dc23
                    2012051166

Dedication

This book is dedicated to two of my very dear, very special friends...
Deborah Stanley and Lacey J. Hill
Quilting brought us together
and to
My sister, Susan O'Riley Stillinger,
My forever best friend

Acknowledgments

I sincerely thank my piecing team—Deborah Stanley, Lacey J. Hill, Debbie Welch, Rebecca Szabo, Nancy Rock, Anna Marie Ameen, Janet Byard, Helle-May Cheney, Lorraine Freed, and Stacey L.D. Moss. You guys are GREAT!

Thank you to my wonderfully talented daughter, Sarah Hahn, who once again contributed her gorgeous quilting designs to the quilts for this book.

I am so very thankful to my dear friend Deborah Stanley, who takes pity on me and gets my quilts bound! I would never have a finished quilt without you!

Thank you to my very special friend Lacey J. Hill, for your cheerleading, your support, your shoulder. You keep me sane.

A very big thank you to Andi Reynolds for her continued guidance and unmatched patience. You are amazing.

Thank you to the talented staff of the American Quilter's Society for making this book come to life. I am so honored to be a part of the AQS family.

Thank you to the folks from Hoffman California; The Electric Quilt Company; The Warm Company; Quilter's Dream Batting; Northcott Silk; Timeless Treasures; Clothworks, Inc.; Elizabeth's Studio, LLC; Superior Threads; Faultless Starch/Bon Ami Company; Sulky, Inc.; Prym Consumer USA; Quilting Possibilities; and Olde City Quilts for providing fabrics and products to make the quilts in this book.

Thank you to the students who have taken New York Beauty Simplified and New York Beauty Diversified classes from me. It's so much fun for me to watch as you discover how easy it is to create these blocks!

Thank you to my husband, Allan, who tolerates it all and never hesitates to jump in where needed!

Contents

THE BASICS

Introduction. 4
Materials and Supplies .4
Foundation Paper .5
Making and Using the Templates 5
Choosing Fabrics 6
Adding Borders. 8
Quilting 8
General Hints 10

THE BLOCKS

New York Beauty .11
Beauty-in-the-Cabin 17
Flower 17
Burst 20
Swirl 23
Square-in-a-Square 25
Beauty-in-a-Square 27

THE QUILTS

Bensonhurst Blooms – Anna Marie Ameen 28
Fire Island Fiesta – Lorraine Freed 32
Tottenville Toads – Linda J. Hahn & Sarah L. Hahn. 36
Niagara Nights 2 – Stacey L. D. Moss 42
Niagara Nights – Linda J. Hahn 45
Midtown Madness – Debbie Welch 46
Saratoga Salsa – Linda J. Hahn. 50
Coney Island Carnival – Linda J. Hahn 54
New Dorp Neutrals – Linda J. Hahn 58
Poughkeepsie Purple – Nancy Rock 62
Moonlight Over Montauk – Janet Byard. 66
Brighton Beach Bazaar – Helle-May Cheney 70
Cocktails in the Catskills – Anna Marie Ameen 10
Buffalo Bubblegum – Rebecca Szabo. 76
Red Red Rochester – Linda J. Hahn 80
Little Red Rochester – Rebecca Szabo. 83
Hues of the Hudson – Sarah L. Hahn 88

RESOURCES 95

ABOUT THE AUTHOR 95

Welcome to Our Pad, 18" x 23½",
made and quilted by Linda J. Hahn

paper piecing

Cover quilt: Coney Island Carnival
Title page quilt: Hues of the Hudson

The Basics

INTRODUCTION

I have been totally thrilled with the success of *New York Beauty Simplified*! As I was designing quilts for that book, I discovered just how versatile the New York Beauty block can be. There were so many more quilts in my head with the only limit being the page count for the book!

Many of the quilts in this book feature blocks that have incorporated the basic New York Beauty block from *Simplified*. Almost all of the blocks can be mixed, matched, and mingled, which will provide you with many more design possibilities.

My teaching style is all about anti-stress and enjoying the process. I have written this book in that style so that you can do just that!

You will be amazed at how quickly and easily the blocks can be constructed. You will use a combination of template-cut fabric shapes and paper foundation-piecing techniques.

It is important that you read through the construction method for each block before you make it, especially if you are already familiar with foundation piecing, as I don't always follow "the rules."

Take your time as you make the first block so you can get the hang of it and become familiar with my way of piecing. The projects are presented in order of complexity, and I know you can make them all.

Enjoy!!

Linda

MATERIALS AND SUPPLIES

The Basics

¼" foot for your machine
Foundation piecing paper
Glue stick (if you are making templates)
Template plastic (if you are making templates)
Invisible tape (to mend foundation paper)
Paper/plastic scissors
Fabric scissors
Pressing surface
Spray starch (I like Magic® Sizing Light)
Iron (I prefer to use a small travel iron)
Small container for cutaways (optional)

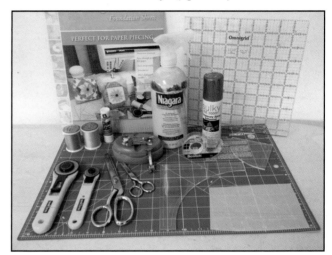

Supply Tips

A 45mm or an 18mm size rotary cutter will work the best. Using the largest blade will not let you get smooth curves, especially on the smaller curves, and the smallest blade will not permit you to create enough pressure to make smooth cuts on the curves.

Ruler placement for the final trim on each block is extremely important. Although you are most welcome to use your favorite ruler, I have found through trial and error that the Omnigrid® 9½" ruler is the easiest to work with. I absolutely LOVE this ruler. If you are using a ruler other than Omnigrid, you may wish to place some ruler tape or masking tape at the measurements so that you can easily see the ruler placement.

When paper piecing, I prefer to use a 50 wt. thread on top (such as MasterPiece™), and a 60 wt. on the bottom (such as The Bottom Line™). Both are from Superior Threads.

The reason for this is that the thread sinks into the seam. At times, you will have the seams crossing over each other. Using a thinner weight thread will cut down on the thread build up over crossed seams. I prefer to piece with neutral color thread (light grey, taupe) in the top and in the bobbin.

And sew ye shall rip. Even the best piecers must rip out at times, so it is expected that you will have to, as well. When ripping with foundation paper, you do not want to attempt to rip from the paper side. If you gently tug apart the pieces you are stitching together and rip from the inside, you will avoid any potential tearing of the paper or making holes in your fabric.

FOUNDATION PAPER

You are more than welcome to use whichever foundation piecing paper you prefer. For the most part, my paper of preference is Electric Quilt® Printable Foundation Sheets. This is because it can be left in the quilt, and after washing, it becomes a layer of polyester.

I use EQ paper for blocks such as New York Beauty and Burst which have smaller pieces. When the foundation pattern has just a few large pieces (such as the Flower block), I use a vellum paper so that I can see the printed pattern on both sides of the paper.

From time to time, there are larger units which necessitate the accuracy foundation piecing provides, but because of the large open areas, you would probably choose to remove the paper. It is perfectly fine to mix up the foundation paper that you are using.

Such is the case with the Flower block. I use EQ paper to piece the Arc foundations, and then use a tear-away paper for the rest of the block.

If you are using foundation paper that must be removed, do not remove it until you have stitched the block into the quilt top. You can spritz the area with water to soften up the paper to make it easier to remove.

Making the Most Out of Foundation Paper

You can make the most out of your foundation paper with careful placement of the pieces on the paper. Make several copies of the foundation pattern pieces in this book—be sure you check the copy sizes against the original.

Arrange pattern pieces on a piece of white copier paper and tape or glue them down. Leave ¼" to ½" extra around each piece. *The goal is to get 2 foundations to sew on from 1 piece of paper whenever possible to conserve paper and save money. Project instructions will read, for example, "50 Regular Arcs. 2 per page = 25 pages."*

Copier Distortion: It Happens

Part of my job as a teacher, author, and designer is to experiment and work out the kinks before sharing with you. I will admit that as we (my daughter Sarah and I) were starting to actually make the quilts in the book, we found ourselves somewhat frustrated with what we eventually discovered to be copier distortion.

Before you begin copying your entire package of foundation paper, make one copy to check for size and copier distortion. In some of the blocks, you will be able to compensate for copier distortion through exact ruler placement as you make your final trim. In other blocks, which require very exact printing, you can simply use another type of paper.

Alternative to Copying Foundations

If you don't have easy access to a copier, you might wish to consider paper-piecing stencils which have been custom cut by Quilting Creations International, Inc., to coordinate with the main blocks from this book. The set is available on my website (see Resources.)

MAKING AND USING THE TEMPLATES

The late Doreen Speckmann shared this method of making templates on a segment of a quilting show on TV many years ago. It works great, and I've been using it ever since.

Make a copy of the background and pie shapes for your block. Do not cut them out. Using a glue stick, lightly cover each piece with glue. Place the template plastic over both pieces and smooth it out. Cut out each piece on the template's solid line.

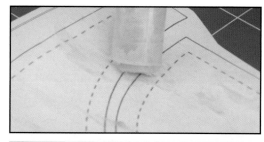

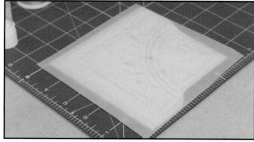

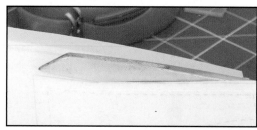

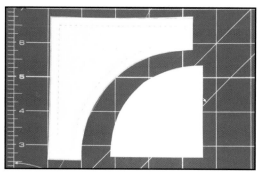

This method eliminates the necessity of tracing and cutting the templates individually.

I recommend that you use a heavy piece of template plastic rather than a lighter weight one since you will be cutting curves.

If you prefer not to make templates, I have had an acrylic version custom made for the pie and background shapes. See Resources for more information.

Either way, trace the template onto the wrong side of the fabric. Remember that the ¼" seam allowance is included, so just sew a ¼" seam along the raw edge.

CHOOSING FABRICS

For some folks, this is the most exciting part of the quilt-making process. For others, it can be the most agonizing. So, let's take the agony out...

The largest blocks in this quilt finish at 8½", and the New York Beauty blocks finish at 6". Each of these blocks has several components pieced into it, so this eliminates using large scale prints (other than for borders). The technique that you will be using is also not conducive to directional prints (unless you are a really good and accurate piecer), stripes, plaids, or novelty prints. Finally, the technique and the size of the pieces are not conducive to fussy cutting.

As you look though the quilts in the book, you will notice that almost all of them have been made using batiks, tone-on-tones, solids, Asian fabrics, and small prints. Any of the color schemes in the sample quilts can be easily interchanged with any of the quilt designs.

I could tell you how to choose fabric the "traditional" way, but you bought this book to learn how I do things.

First and foremost, you do NOT need to be "matchy matchy." Lime green and cheddar/yellow/orange are great "zingers."

If your quilt calls for 5 fabrics, walk around the quilt shop and choose 6–8 fabrics that you really like. Pile them on top of each other and walk away about 10 feet, turn around, and look. Pull out the ones that look way too dark and way too light. Are there any fabrics that are way too busy? Is the print too big on any of them?

If you have chosen one print and the rest solids, does the print look out of place? Or is it just the right touch, lending much-needed texture?

Have your quilt pattern in one hand and look at the fabrics. I like to put my favorite fabric in the most prominent position in the block or as the major fabric in the block that has the most pieces to it.

Choosing a particular fabric collection that you like is another way to select fabrics. For example, the quilt Red Red Rochester (page 80) was made using fabrics from one particular collection. In this fashion, you know the fabrics will coordinate; you just need to place them into the design elements.

These fabrics are from the LaBelle collection by Northcott Silk, Inc.

Mentally place each fabric in a location in the design and pull it out of the pile. I usually bring some sticky notes and stick them on the fabric with the appropriate yardage for the color.

A fun exercise to do is to go to a quilt shop with a friend, exchange patterns, and pick each other's fabrics. You may end up using fabrics or colors that you wouldn't have thought about using before. Another way to choose fabrics for a quilt is to bring a man or child along with you; they are usually way less inhibited.

Surprises are great! Don't agonize over choosing fabric.

Quilt Yardage

We ALL make cutting errors, and sometimes fabrics shrink after washing. I have taken this into consideration when calculating yardage requirements for the projects in this book, so my yardage calculations are generous. When I am purchasing yardage, I always buy an extra ⅛ to ¼ yard—JUST IN CASE!

Yardage is calculated based on 40" usable width of fabric. The yardage stated for backing fabric assumes that you are machine quilting the quilt (and allows for some extra) AND also provides enough fabric for you to have a matching 4" hanging sleeve. If you do not wish to have a matching sleeve, please reduce the yardage by ¼ yard.

The sizes of the pieces that I have provided are what I work with and pretty much guarantee that you won't have to rip out or reposition.

The backing yardage assumes that you will be piecing the back together with a vertical seam and also includes enough yardage for you to make a matching 4" hanging sleeve (quilt shows usually require this size sleeve).

Binding fabric yardage is calculated for 2½" wide straight of grain strips.

Conserving Fabrics

As you are cutting out some shapes (such as the Background shape), you may find that you have a very usable scrap of fabric left over. Don't hesitate to use this piece to cut other shapes.

Don't throw out any sizeable scraps until you are completely done with the quilt. Sometimes you may find yourself a mere 2" x 2" short to complete your project. Rather than run out to the quilt shop to purchase a minimum ¼ yard cut, I just piece scraps together and then cut out the size that I need.

ADDING BORDERS

One of the many hats that I wear in the quilting industry is that of a longarm quilter. One of my biggest pet peeves is seeing beautiful quilts come across the machine with "wonky" borders. I can tell immediately whether a customer has measured and applied his or her borders properly. Quilt show judges are likewise able to spot this. In the name of beautiful, straight quilts everywhere, here are my border tips:

First, I heavily starch my borders before applying them to the inner quilt. This will help a little, especially if the fabric is cut on the bias.

Another help: I cut my borders along the straight of grain out of the required yardage first, and then cut the patchwork pieces out of what is left.

Everyone has a preference over which border to add first. My preference is to add the side borders first, and then the top and bottom borders, like this:

1) Measure YOUR quilt from raw edge to raw edge through the center of the top. The reason that you measure through the center is because sometimes the sides of the quilt will stretch during the piecing process. Plus, not everyone stitches a perfect ¼" seam and not everyone is a perfect piecer, *thus, the border cutting dimensions in books like this one are suggestions, not rules.*

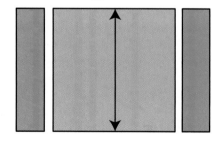

2) Cut the side borders to your measurement—this may or may not differ slightly from the cutting instructions in the pattern. Attach by folding the border and quilt top in half, pinching each one to create a center mark, and pinning the center of the border to the center of the top, right sides together. Then pin the ends of the border to the ends of the quilt.

As you pin the distance between the center and each end, you will be able to ease in any differences. If you notice any fullness, sew with the side with the most fullness against the feed dogs to help with easing.

3) Once the side borders are attached and seams are pressed toward the border fabric, measure the quilt across the center from raw edge to raw edge, including the side borders. Cut the top and bottom borders to this measurement and attach them in the same way.

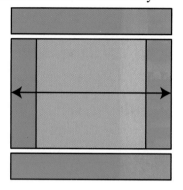

If you need to piece the borders, I recommend that you do so using a diagonal seam as opposed to a straight seam; this will distribute the seam allowance bulk.

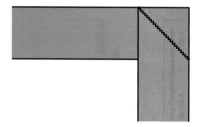

QUILTING

The quilting designs that you use in your quilt can add dimension and bring your quilt to life! I am well aware that "quilt as desired" are words that can make a quilter cringe!

My 21-year old daughter, Sarah, quilted many of the quilts in the book (and charged me!). She has shared her original designs with you, but note that sometimes the quilting on the sample quilt and her designs are different. This is to give you more suggestions and options! The design elements can be mixed and matched between the quilt blocks. For example, you may like the Spire design from one quilt and the Pie design from another.

Having the right supplies can make a huge difference in the end result of your quilting. Every quilter and quilt teacher has their own preferences when it comes to specific supplies and products. I will share mine with you:

Batting

You will be much more successful with the quilts in this book when using 100 percent cotton or a cotton/poly blend batting. These quilts are not meant to be fluffy.

Basting

Even though I am a longarm quilter, there are times when I use my domestic machine for quilting. I am a very big fan of spray basting, and for this I use a Sulky® adhesive called KK2000. It is environmentally friendly and works quickly. Spray the batting, not the fabric. There is no need to use a heavy hand when spraying. You want the batting just wet enough to make it tacky to hold the top in place.

Needle

I use a 90/14 Topstitch needle for piecing and for quilting and change it to a new one for every project.

Thread

I am admittedly a "threadaholic." I love looking at the various shades and colors on thread racks. I especially love variegated threads, as I think using them gives the quilts extra dimension.

I quilt with a 30wt. or 40wt. variegated thread on top (such as Superior Threads King Tut™ thread or Sulky® Blendables® thread) and a coordinating thread in the bobbin, such as Superior Threads The Bottom Line™ thread.

Backing

The best advice I can give you regarding quilt backs is to let loose and HAVE SOME FUN! There is no rule that says you must have a back that matches the front of the quilt. After investing a fair amount of money and a good amount of work into your *New York Beauty Diversified* quilt, you most certainly don't want to put plain old boring muslin on the back.

The backs of my quilts tell stories or make statements. For example, the name of our business is "Frog Hollow Designs," so when I make quilts for a magazine or fabric company, I try to put a frog fabric on the back. You might see pirates, martinis, or palm trees on the backs of some quilts (I like to cruise the Caribbean). You can use fabrics that share a special story with the recipient of the quilt (to recall a love of baseball or commemorate a casino trip, for example). Also, a busy back will hide tension imperfections and starts and stops.

It's so much fun to watch people's expressions when I turn a quilt and they see the fun backing!

Auditioning Quilting Designs

If you are comfortable with free-motion meandering, you will be able to accomplish any of the quilting designs in the book. I recommend that you practice a little bit to train your mental muscle.

To do this, make a copy of the black-and-white blank image of the block or quilt that you will be quilting. Slide the copy into a clear page protector. Use a dry-erase marker to audition and practice your chosen design elements.

Try different quilting elements in various areas of the quilt block until you are happy with the design. Working this way will also help you develop a quilting plan so that you can minimize stops and starts.

Another alternative is to use a quilting stencil designed specifically for the New York Beauty block and a pounce pad (see Resources, page 95).

GENERAL HINTS

Stitch Length

When paper piecing, you may wish to shorten your stitch length a bit. You don't want the stitches too tight—just a smidgen tighter than what you would normally sew with. Remember, you just might have to rip them out!!

Starching and Pressing

In making the quilts in this book, starched is good—crispy is better. I am continually starching my fabrics and blocks throughout the piecing process. This will help keep the pieces from stretching or distorting and will also help make finger pressing possible.

I chain piece whenever feasible. As I cut the pieces apart, I place them on the ironing surface and spritz them with starch (and do not press), so the starch can dry while I work on other pieces.

Press—do NOT iron.

Do NOT use steam in the block construction process.

Iron Gunk

After heavy starching, you may find that your iron has accumulated some gunk on the soleplate. Not removing the gunk may result in it being transferred to the next item being ironed at the most inopportune moment, such as when your husband is trying to press his own shirt when he is late for work. To remove gunk, iron a used dryer sheet with a hot iron.

The Piecing Factor

Everyone has their own personal thoughts when it comes to piecing. One person may choose to rip out a seam if their intersection is one thread off while another person may choose not to. I respect both choices and all in between. I am not the best piecer in the world and I don't enter shows competitively, so I am not as meticulous as one might be if making a show quilt. I'm all about enjoying the process.

Rotary Cutter

You will be cutting curves so it's important to start with a new blade to get the cleanest cut possible.

How to Design Using Mix and Match Blocks

Most of the blocks in this book can be mixed and matched. The New York Beauty blocks all finish at 6".

Make copies of the individual blocks in the book. If you like, you can color them prior to making copies. Cut them out and begin placing them on your design wall until you come up with a design that you would like to make. Refer to the cutting requirements that are required for each block, and with simple math, you will be able to calculate the fabrics needed for your quilt.

COCKTAILS IN THE CATSKILLS, 37½" x 37½", made by Anna Marie Ameen, Princeton Junction, New Jersey. Quilted by the author.
See BRIGHTON BEACH BAZAAR on page 70.

The Blocks

NEW YORK BEAUTY BLOCK

To make a New York Beauty block you will need these fabric pieces: Pie, Arc, (also called Regular Arc, Solid Arc, Spire Arc, or Split Spire Arc, depending on what it looks like), and Background. Note: The Arcs, except for the Solid type, are pieced. The two pointy or sharp pieces are called Spire and Background Spire. Together they form an Arc foundation.

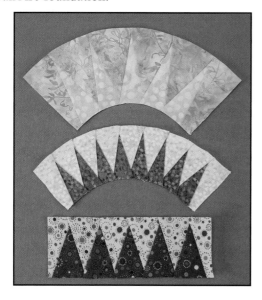

Use templates to make Pies, Solid Arcs, and Backgrounds. Note that Pies and Backgrounds may be one piece or split into two pieces.

Use foundation paper piecing to create the Regular/Spire Arcs (no piecing needed for Solid Arcs).

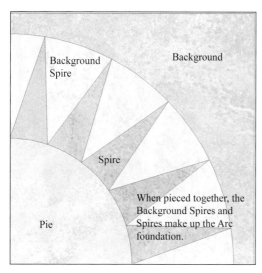

Background Spire

Background

Spire

Pie

When pieced together, the Background Spires and Spires make up the Arc foundation.

The templates and piecing patterns in this book make 6" finished New York Beauty blocks. You will sometimes add fabric to the basic block to make new blocks (see pages 17–27). These will finish at 8½".

The technique we're going to work on is WAY out of the box, and if you'll work through it slowly, you'll be virtually guaranteed a perfect block every time. Ready??? Take a breath and let's begin.

Cutting Pie and Background Shapes

Don't skip over this section! The ease of the technique depends a lot upon this step. I would suggest that you cut and make one test block to determine what your personal measurement will be. Let me explain...

Place the Background template on an 8" square of fabric. For the first block, leave approximately ½" extra on the straight edges of the template only. As we move further along on the block construction, you will see how this extra ½" works. You may have to add a little more, or you may be able to reduce this measurement a bit. This will be your personal measurement.

Cut the curve right to the template.

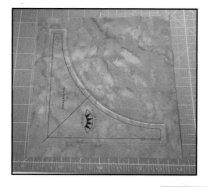

Fabric Saving Tip:
You can cut a Pie shape
out of the other side of
the fabric if you choose.

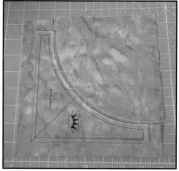

The Pie shape is cut the same way. Leave approximately ½" on the straight edges of the template. Cut right to the curved edge on the template.

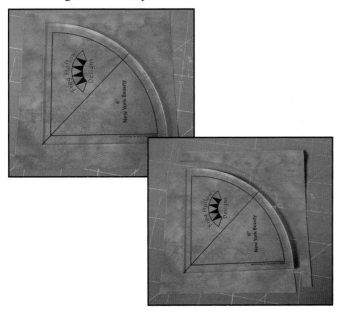

Piecing the Arc Foundations

You will be using the same technique to create most of the variations of the blocks that are featured in this book, whether curved or straight. Please read over the entire process before beginning to piece the Arcs. The process is the same whether you are piecing an Arc foundation or a Spire Strip.

Note: The photos show piecing with brightly colored thread for ease of visibility. You should piece with a neutral color thread on top and in the bobbin.

Copy the designated number of Arc foundations onto your choice of foundation paper. You can fit 2 or 3 Arc foundations on each page.

Cut the foundations apart leaving ¼" (more or less) away from the outermost line. You don't have to be "on the money" with your cutting to get exactly ¼"—just leave a little extra.

If you are using translucent foundation paper, you will be able to see both sides of the printing and it will not make a difference which side is the "right" side and which side is the "wrong" side. If you are using plain copier paper or a foundation paper that is not translucent, the printed (copied) side of the paper is the "right" side. It will be the side that faces you as you stitch.

You will begin your piecing on the first diagonal line—not on the straight lines on the edge of the foundation paper.

Lay the foundation paper in front of you so that the Spire lines are horizontal. Pick up the short edge of the paper closest to you and roll the paper away from you until you see the first diagonal line. Finger crease the paper. This will be your placement guide.

Lay the foundation paper back in the same orientation. Place a rectangular piece of Background Spire fabric over the folded line by approximately ¼". Insert a pin to hold the fabric in place on the foundation paper. Now, take one of the Spire rectangles and place that raw edge to raw edge over the Background fabric, right sides together. Switch the pin to hold both rectangles to the foundation paper. Don't pin on the sewing line!

I tell my students to always have the excess foundation away from them and the excess fabric toward them to make sure that they are placing the fabrics correctly.

Turn the piece over to the wrong side of the foundation paper and stitch on the diagonal line. Stitch from edge to edge, i.e., cover this line from one end to the other. You do not have to backstitch.

Remove the foundation unit from your sewing machine. Finger press the fabrics open or press with an iron (whatever your pleasure). If you have heavily starched your fabrics, a finger press will crease them just fine.

Place the Arc foundation in a vertical position with the Background Spire closest to you and the excess foundation paper facing away from you. Roll both the foundation paper and the fabric away from you to the next diagonal line. If you work in this fashion, you will not miss the next line to sew. Finger crease the next line.

Lay the Arc foundation back down on the table, again with the fabric closest to you and the excess paper away from you. Place a Spire fabric approximately ¼" over the creased line. Note that the piece will be on a slight diagonal. Flip over and stitch.

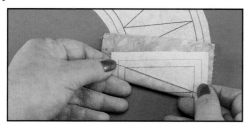

You will now begin trimming the excess fabric from underneath the sewn piece. Do not unfold the piece you just stitched yet—fold the foundation paper back so that you do not cut it. Cut the excess fabric away approximately ⅛" to ¼" away from the stitched line.

Note: If you are using light fabrics, you will need to check to see if there is any shadowing on your Arc foundation. If there is, you will need to grade the seam. This means that you will cut the seams of the Background Spire and Spire separately, cutting one shorter than the other so that you cannot see the darker fabric shadowing through.

Continue stitching, flipping, and trimming until the entire Arc foundation is pieced.

Fabric Saver Hint: If you are careful when you place the first Background Spire piece, you can trim it at any time during your piecing process and use the cutaway as the last Background Spire piece.

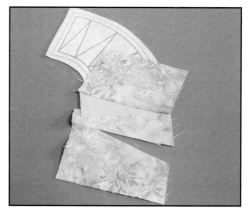

Trim the Arc foundation to the outermost line on the **curved edges only**. Leave approximately ¼" beyond the outermost line on the **straight edges only**. Leaving the extra fabric on the straight edges will help in compensating in the event of copier distortion. You will see the reason for this when we do the final trim.

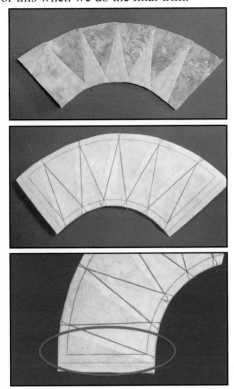

Setting in the Pie Shape

Work with the Arc foundation and the Pie shape first. Stitch with the Pie shape ON TOP of the Arc foundation. The reason for this is that you can now IGNORE the stitching lines on the Arc foundation. It is more important that you get a smooth line than it is to stitch on the line.

Before you start—is the Pie shape starched and crispy? If not, please starch it now. Fold the Arc foundation and the Pie shape in half and make a crease in the center of each. Pin the two pieces together.

Pull the left side of the Pie shape to the left side of the Arc foundation. Allow the Pie shape to extend approximately ¼" beyond the edge of the Arc foundation. Insert a pin to hold the pieces in that orientation.

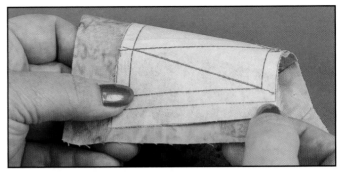

Begin stitching with the Pie shape on top. Take a few stitches and then remove the end pin. Take a few more stitches, and you will be able to now remove the center pin. (No more pins!)

You will see that the Pie shape raw edge will line up with the raw edge of the Arc foundation for only a few stitch lengths. That's fine. You will need to raise your presser foot and reposition the Pie fabric every 3–4 stitches. Don't stretch the Pie shape—it will fit perfectly if you stitch slowly and reposition every few stitches. Some people only take 2–3 stitches before they reposition, some may take more.

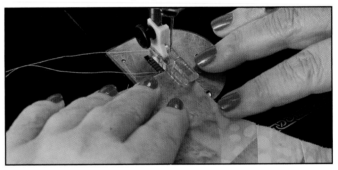

When you have completed stitching the Pie shape onto the Arc foundation, it should look like this—DO NOT trim anything yet. Hang in there; there is one more piece to go.

If there are any puckers, before you unsew, try the following:

- Tear the Arc foundation paper behind the pucker and touch the pucker with the tip of an iron.
- Spray starch the pucker and touch it with the tip of an iron.

Setting in the Background Shape

Phew, that was the harder of the 2 pieces to set in. This next piece goes on much easier.

Before you start this step—did you starch the Background piece? If not, please starch it before you begin.

As before, fold the Background piece and the Arc foundation in half and crease. (Hint: The point of the middle Spire is the Arc foundation's middle). Place the Background piece on top of the Arc foundation, align the centers, and insert a pin. Note: If you're working with a double Arc, as in RED RED ROCHESTER, the same applies—the Background piece goes on top.

Gently, without stretching, walk your fingers toward the left edge, aligning the raw edges. You will see there's an overlap of approximately ¼" to ½"—that's fine. Insert a pin at the end, leaving the overlap.

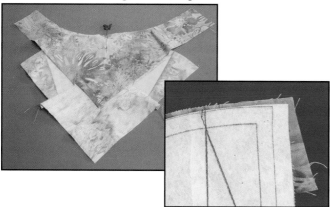

Place the pieces under the sewing machine foot and take a few stitches. Remove the first pin. Continue attaching the Background piece, aligning the raw edges as you go. Once you have done this a few times, you will be able to stitch the entire Background piece onto the Arc foundation without having to lift the presser foot.

Your completed block should look like this...

Yes, like that. Depending on how much overlap you allowed, you may see even more distortion. Not to worry, all will be revealed.

The Final Trim

Get ready for the WOW!

Position your block with the Spires pointing up and to the right.

Place your ruler on top of the block and place the 3/4" line of the ruler in the seam allowance between the Arc foundation and the Background shape at both the top and the right side of the block.

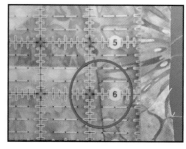

The next measurement you will look at is to make sure that the diagonal line on the ruler goes through the BOTTOM center of the center Spire. Copier distortion may have the line going slightly to the left or slightly to the right of the point of the center Spire. This is OK.

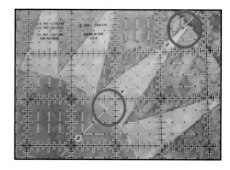

The block will be 6½" unfinished, so the last ruler placement that you need to be aware of is that there should be ¼" from the bottom of the last spire to the 6½" line on the ruler that will permit you to stitch the blocks together.

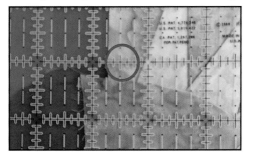

WOW!

The final trim measurements are also applicable to the Split Spire Arc. The final trim for the Solid Arc can be found in the instructions for BRIGHTON BEACH BAZAAR.

Piecing the Blocks Together

When I piece the New York Beauty blocks together (or any of the other blocks that you will find in this book), I have a different piecing method.

Rather than pin with the point going into (toward) the block, I place the pins with the points going to the outside of the block and have the point of the pin coming out ¼" from the edge of the block. This allows you to keep the pins in the block while you stitch them together.

If you pin with the points going into (toward) the block and you pull out the pin prior to stitching over it, the blocks might shift slightly and the seams may be a thread or two off.

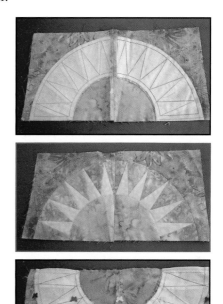

When pressing foundation-pieced blocks, I press the seams open to distribute the bulk of the fabric and foundation.

BEAUTY-IN-THE-CABIN BLOCK
(8½" finished)

For this block, use your choice of the Regular Arc or the Split Spire Arc. The New York Beauty part of the block should be 6½" unfinished.

Note: Press all seams toward the log.

Position the New York Beauty block with the spires pointing up and to the top right. Add a 1¾" x 6½" log to the right side.

Add a 1¾" x 8" log of the same fabric across the top of the block.

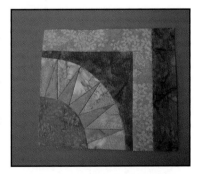

Position the block with the spires pointing up and to the top right. Add a 1¾" x 8" log of the next color to the right side.

Finish the block by adding a 1¾" x 9" log that is the same color as log #3 across the top.

FLOWER BLOCK
(8½" finished)

Use your choice of the Regular Arc or the Split Spire Arc for this block. Either one should be 6½" unfinished before adding background pieces.

You can use the foundation paper of your choice for the flower part of the block. Since there are just a few large pieces, I use translucent vellum paper and remove it later.

Each 8½" finished block requires the following pieces:

Background: 1 rectangle 3½" x 9"
              1 rectangle 3½" x 7"

Stem/Leaves: 1 square 5" x 5" cut in half on the diagonal
              1 rectangle 3" x 7½"
              1 rectangle 2½" x 4½"

Cut out the foundation paper and lay it out next to your sewing machine to make sure that you are working on the correct side.

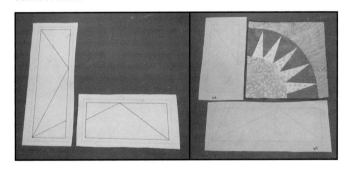

You will be following the technique for basic foundation piecing which can be found on pages 11–14.

Lay the background fabric pieces over the appropriate foundation piece. Roll and fold the foundation piece to indicate placement. Place one of the triangles cut from the 5" square over the larger corner of each piece. Stitch from the outermost line to the outermost line. Fold and trim.

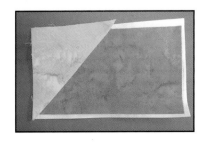

Roll and fold the opposite corner of the smaller background foundation. Place the 2½" x 5½" rectangle over the folded line. Stitch from the outermost line to the outermost line. Fold and trim to the outermost line. This piece should now measure 2½" x 6½".

Roll and fold the larger background to the next line. Place the 3" x 8" rectangle over the folded line. Stitch from the outermost line to the outermost line. Fold back and trim closely to the stitching line. Do not discard the cutaway of the background fabric, as this is the next piece to sew.

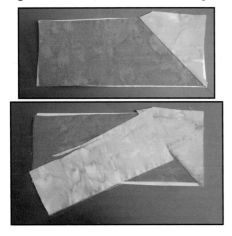

Roll and fold the larger background piece to the next line. Place the piece of background fabric that you just cut away over the folded line. Stitch from the outermost line to the outermost line.

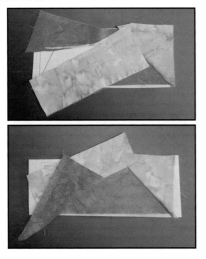

Trim each piece to the outermost line using scissors or a rotary cutter.

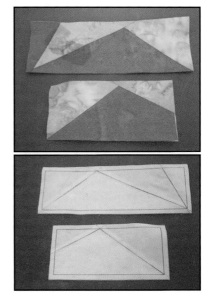

Place your chosen New York Beauty block next to your sewing machine with the spires pointing up and to the right.

Stitch the smaller foundation piece to one side of the New York Beauty block. Press to the New York Beauty block or press open.

Carefully pin the larger foundation piece to the bottom side of the New York Beauty block. Stitch on the line of the foundation paper.

Open the block up and press the seam open or toward the foundation. This block should measure 9" unfinished.

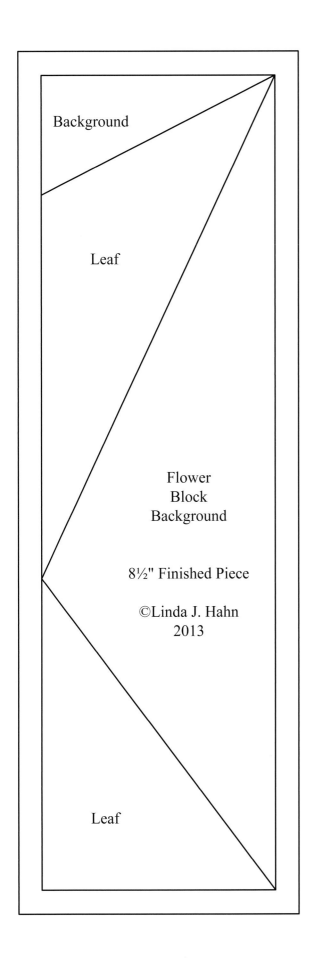

FLOWER BLOCK

Use 1 of each piece per block.

Background

Leaf

Flower
Block
Background

8½" Finished Piece

©Linda J. Hahn
2013

Leaf

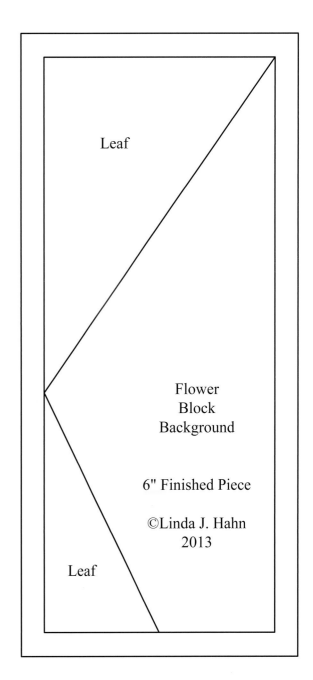

Leaf

Flower
Block
Background

6" Finished Piece

©Linda J. Hahn
2013

Leaf

BURST BLOCK

The Burst block is made in 4 triangular sections that are joined together to make the Burst. You will note in the pattern that the Spires do not go all the way to the inner line. This is so you will have approximately ½" from the edge of the Spires to the cutting line to ensure that you are not cutting off any points during the final trim.

You will need:
4 foundation patterns per burst

Center: 4 background rectangles 3" x 3½"
Spires: 16 rectangles 2" x 4½"
Background: 4 squares 4½" cut in half on the diagonal
Background: 8 rectangles 2" x 5"
Center Triangles: 2 squares 5" cut in half on the diagonal

Place the 3" x 3½" rectangle over the center Background portion of the foundation and pin away from the stitching lines.

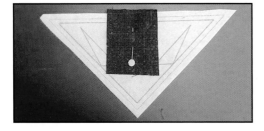

Fold for placement and stitch the first Spire.

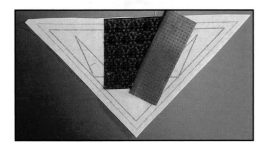

Repeat on the opposite side with another Spire rectangle.

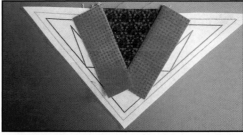

Fold for placement and add one of the Background triangles.

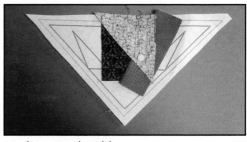

Repeat on the opposite side.

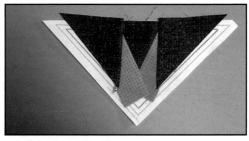

The next piece to add is a Spire fabric.

Repeat on the opposite side.

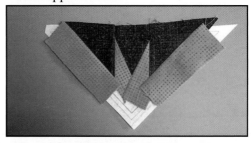

Add the 2" x 5" Background rectangle.

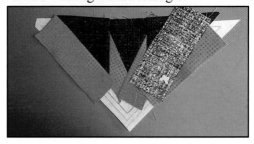

Repeat on the opposite side. Press.

Add the center triangle to the bottom of this unit.

Flip the block so that the paper side is facing you. Place the ruler so that the diagonal ¼" lines on the ruler are placed on the inner line of the foundation pattern. Cut on two sides only. Do not trim across the top of the Spires.

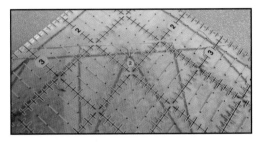

Flip the block back so that it is right side up. Lift the triangle portion up and cut away the fabric and the foundation leaving approximately ¼".

Do not trim the top edge of this triangle; this trim is done during the final trim after the units are stitched into the block.

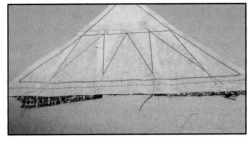

Stitch the triangle sections together into halves, and the halves into a whole block.

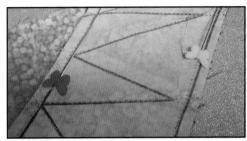

This block was designed so that there is more than ¼" extra from the edge of the Spires to the raw edge of the block. You may find that if you mark some seam allowance lines with chalk, it will be easier to trim your block.

The 4½" line on the ruler should go between the middle spires on the top and the right. In a perfect world, the diagonal line should be on the seam allowance. Trim to 9" x 9".

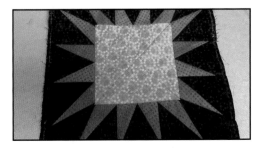

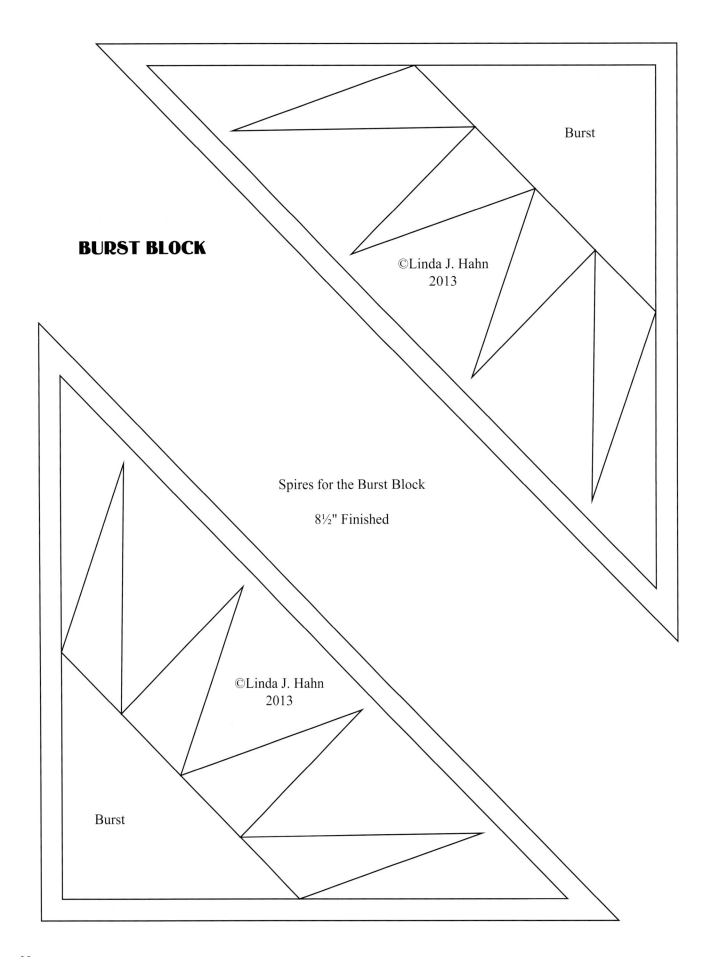

BURST BLOCK

Burst

©Linda J. Hahn
2013

Spires for the Burst Block

8½" Finished

©Linda J. Hahn
2013

Burst

SWIRL BLOCK
(8½" finished)

You may use either regular paper foundation or Electric Quilt Foundation paper for this block. Each 8½" finished Swirl block requires 4 copies of the pattern on page 24.

Cut 4 rectangles 3" x 6" (piece A)
Cut 4 rectangles 3" x 6" (piece B)
Cut 4 rectangles 2½" x 4½" (piece C)
Cut 4 rectangles 2½" x 6½" (piece D)
Cut 4 squares 2½" x 2½" (piece E)

I recommend laying out your foundation pieces next to your sewing machine to make sure that you will be piecing on the correct side. Before you begin, check to be sure that the block pieces are in the proper orientation. Follow the letter sequence to sew.

Using the basic instructions for foundation piecing on pages 12–13, place a 3" x 6" fabric piece on the foundation. Fold to crease, and then place a 3" x 6" piece of the next fabric face down on it. Stitch from the outermost line to the outermost line.

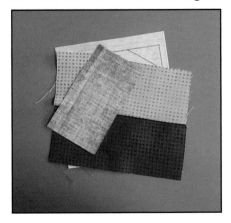

Fold to crease and add a 2½" x 4½" rectangle.

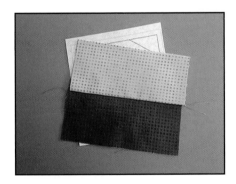

Fold, crease, and add the 2½" x 6½" rectangle. Cut away the excess.

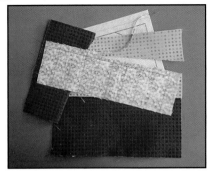

Fold, crease, and add the 2½" square.

Turn the block over and trim on the outermost lines. This piece should measure 5" unfinished.

Pin as shown and stitch two units together along the seam line of the pattern piece. The horizontal pins are pinned through the seam line. The vertical pin is also pinned through the seam line, but it will be removed as you stitch. Press the seam open or to one side. Repeat for the remaining two units.

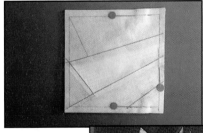

Stitch the two units together to form the block. Press the seams open or to one side. The block should measure 9" unfinished.

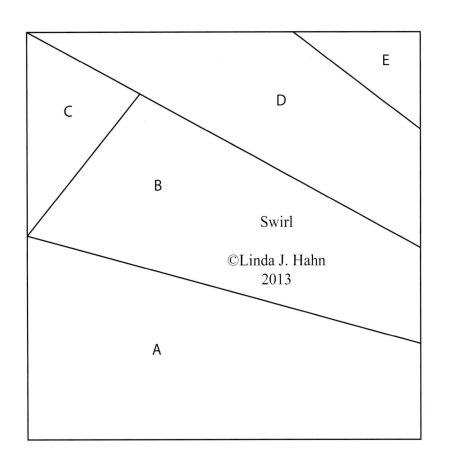

C

D

E

B

Swirl

©Linda J. Hahn
2013

A

SWIRL BLOCK

Use 4 Foundations for
1 Swirl Block

8½" Finished

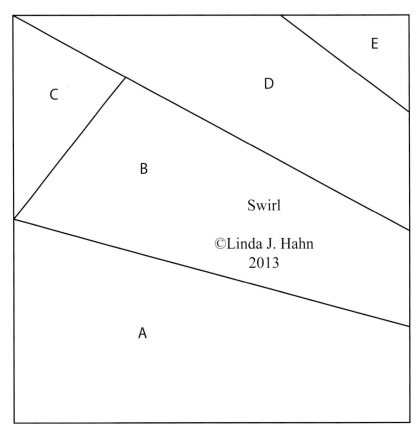

C

D

E

B

Swirl

©Linda J. Hahn
2013

A

SQUARE-IN-A-SQUARE BLOCK
(8½" finished)

This is a different way of making the Square-in-a-Square block. The inner portion of the block is foundation pieced. The last round of triangles is added without the foundation to eliminate bulk. This block can be used with either type of foundation paper (leave-in or tear-out).

You will need:
Center: 3½" square
Round 1: 2 squares 4" x 4" cut in half on the diagonal
Round 2: 2 squares 5" x 5" cut in half on the diagonal
Round 3: 2 squares 6½" x 6½" cut in half on the diagonal

Center the 3½" square over the center portion of the foundation. Place a pin in the center. Turn the foundation over and take a peek to make sure that the square extends over the stitching lines.

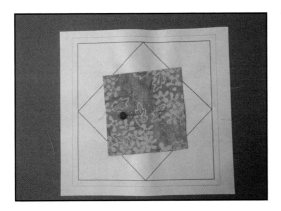

Fold for placement and make a crease.

Place a Round 1 triangle face down on the square, raw edges matching. Flip and stitch on the line. Trim the excess fabric from the seam allowance to approximately ⅛" to ¼".

Repeat on the opposite side, and then add the remaining two sides to complete Round 1. Press the seam toward the point of the triangle.

Repeat the process using the Round 2 triangles.

Trim the square on the outermost line to 6½" unfinished.

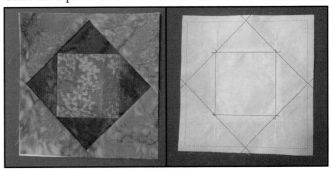

Add the 6½" Round 3 triangles.

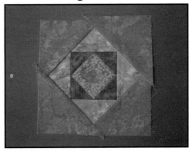

Trim the block to 9" by placing the 4½" lines on the ruler at the seam intersections on the top and the right side. Trim, then rotate the block and trim to 9".

SQUARE-IN-A-SQUARE BLOCK

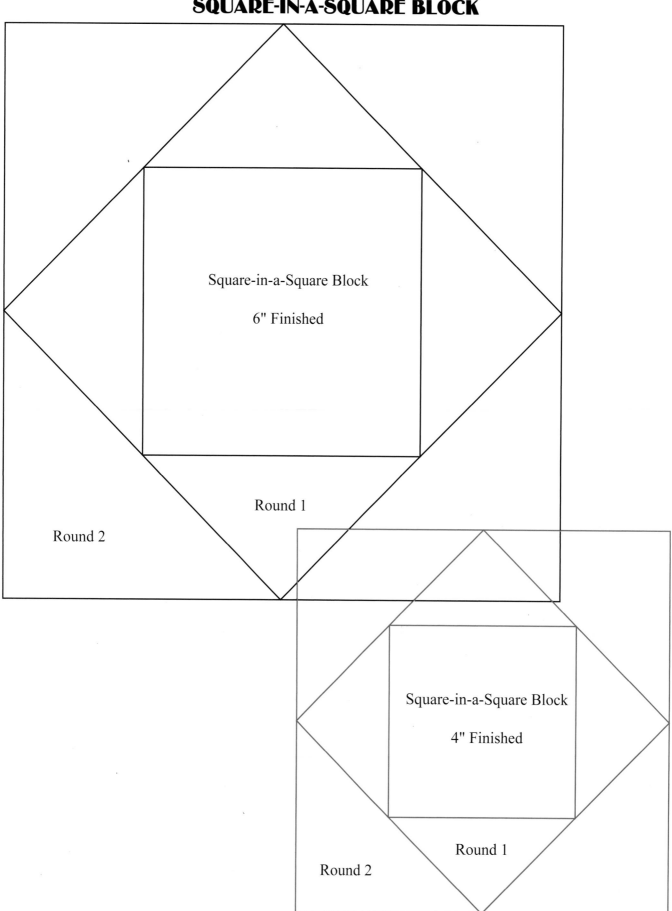

Square-in-a-Square Block

6" Finished

Round 1

Round 2

Square-in-a-Square Block

4" Finished

Round 1

Round 2

BEAUTY-IN-A-SQUARE BLOCK
(8½" finished)

You will need your choice of a 6" finished New York Beauty block and two 7" squares cut in half on the diagonal. Some of the quilts in this book use 1 color and some use 2 colors, so make sure that you refer to the correct quilt photograph for your desired color placement.

The block is assembled and trimmed exactly as Square-in-a-Square, which can be found on page 25.

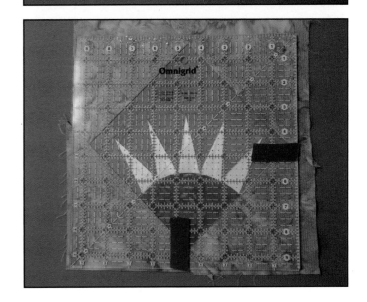

BENSONHURST BLOOMS, 55" x 35". Made by Anna Marie Ameen, Princeton Junction, New Jersey. Quilted by the author.

Bensonhurst

BLOOMS

Have fun mixing, matching, and intermingling the fabrics for this quilt! When you look at the photo of the quilt, you will see that the fabrics gradate to create the "flowers in a field" effect.

Blocks You Will Make

36 Regular Arc New York Beauty blocks (page 11)

Foundations You Will Need

- 36 Regular Arcs (template on page 93). Use any foundation paper. 2 per page = 18 pages.

Fabrics

- **Yellow**: ⅛ yard
    Cut: 24 rectangles 3" x 4" (Sun Spires)

- **Orange**: ¼ yard
    Cut 20 rectangles 2½" x 3½" (Sun Background Spires)

- **Light orange**: ⅛ yard
    Cut 4 squares 4½" x 4½" (Sun Pies)

- **Light blue**: 1 yard
    Cut 8 squares 8" x 8" (Sky)
    Cut 24 rectangles 3" x 4". Cut some of these from the leftovers of the 8" squares. (Background Spires)
    Cut 6 squares 6½" x 6½" in half on the diagonal. (Backgrounds)

- **Assorted greens** to total 1¼ yards (Pies, Spires, and Backgrounds. Mix and match between blocks.)
    Cut 6 squares 6½" x 6½" in half on the diagonal (Corner Triangles)
    Cut 11 squares 4½" x 4½"
    Cut 55 rectangles 2½" x 3½"
    Cut 36 rectangles 3" x 4"
    Cut 6 squares 8" x 8"

- **Assorted florals** to total 2 yards (Use fat quarters or ⅛ yards for best variety. The more the merrier!)
    Cut 21 squares 4" x 4" (Pies)
    Cut 105 rectangles 2½" x 3½" (Spires)
    Cut 126 rectangles 3" x 4" (Background Spires)
    Cut 21 squares 8" x 8" (Backgrounds)

- **Backing and matching hanging sleeve:** 2⅔ yards
    2 cuts of 32" x 43" each, pieced vertically

- **Batting:** 63" x 43"

- **Binding:** ½ yard

Sewing

Make:

- 6 New York Beauty blocks all green.

- 4 New York Beauty yellow/orange blocks for the sun.

- 5 New York Beauty blocks with a green Pie, green Spires, and a floral Background.

- 4 New York Beauty blocks with floral Pies and Spires and blue Background Spires and Background.

- 4 New York Beauty blocks with a blue Background.

- Make the remaining 13 New York Beauty blocks in a variety of intermingled florals.

Lay your quilt out on the floor or design wall and arrange the blocks until you are pleased with the look. This quilt is stitched together in diagonal rows.

Quilt, bind, label, and enjoy!

Quilt Assembly

Quilting Design

Fire Island Fiesta, 60" x 60". Designed and made by Lorraine Freed, Harrison, New York. Quilted by the author.

Fire Island

FIESTA

Here's how to achieve a very dramatic effect using only three fabrics. The sample quilt was quilted using the Fascination pantograph pattern from Lorien Quilting.

Blocks You Will Make
- 40 Regular Arc New York Beauty blocks (page 11)
- 24 Alternate blocks (see right)

Foundations You Will Need
- 40 Regular Arcs (template on page 93). Use EQ paper.
  2 templates per page = 20 pages.

Fabrics
- **Black:** 2 yards
  Cut 40 squares 4½" x 4½" (Pies)
  Cut 24 squares 4" x 4" (Alternate blocks)
  Cut 2 strips 3" x 54½" (Border)
  Cut 2 strips 3" x 60" (Border)
  Cut 6 strips 2½" x width of fabric (Binding)

- **Black on red print:** 3½ yards
  Cut 40 squares 8" x 8" (Background)
  Cut 200 rectangles 2½" x 3½" (Spires)
  Cut 12 squares 7" x 7" (Alternate blocks)

- **Black on white print:** 3 yards
  Cut 12 squares 7¼" x 7¼" (Alternate blocks)
  Cut 2 strips 4½" x 54½" strips (Border)
  Cut 2 strips 4½" x 48½" strips (Border)
  Cut 240 retangles 3" x 4" (Background Spires)

- **Backing and matching hanging sleeve:** 4 yards
  2 cuts of 40" x 68" each, pieced vertically

- **Batting:** 68" x 68"

- **Binding:** ½ yard included in Black yardage

Sewing
Make:
- 40 New York Beauty blocks.

- 24 Fire Island Fiesta Alternate blocks.

Follow the assembly diagram on page 34 to construct the top.

Add borders (page 8).

Quilt, bind, label, and enjoy!

Alternate Block for Fire Island Fiesta
Make half-square triangles: Place two 7" squares right sides together. Draw a diagonal line from corner to corner. Stitch ¼" away on each side of the drawn line. Cut the triangles apart on the drawn line and press toward the darker of the two fabrics.

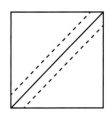

Draw a diagonal line from corner to corner on the 4" squares. Place one of the 4" squares on the corner of the half-square triangle. Make sure that the diagonal line is going in the same direction as the orientation of the block.

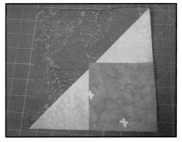

Stitch directly on the drawn line. Trim away the right hand side of the 4" triangle that you just stitched.

Press the remaining half of the triangle over so that its raw edges meet the raw edges of the underlying block.

Quilt Assembly

Quilting Design

TOTTENVILLE TOADS, 64" x 64". Pieced, appliquéd, and quilted by Linda J. Hahn and Sarah L. Hahn.

Tottenville

TOADS

Tottenville is a section of Staten Island where I was born and grew up. Tottenville High School was the football rival of my high school—New Dorp. (See my tribute to New Dorp High School on page 59.) Our company name is Frog Hollow Designs, so Sarah and I designed and made this piece to represent our business.

Blocks You Will Make

• 50 New York Beauty blocks with Regular Arcs (page 11)

Foundations You Will Need

• 50 Regular Arcs (template on page 93). Use EQ paper.
    2 per page = 25 pages.
• Frog pattern (page 39)
• Lily Pad patterns (as many as you like; page 40)
• 2 yards of your favorite fusible web

Fabrics

• **Blue:** 3½ yards
    Cut 50 squares 8" x 8" (Backgrounds)
    Cut 30 squares 6½" x 6½" (Alternate blocks)

• **Greens #1:** A total of 5 yards (Blocks). Choose a nice variety of lights, mediums, and darks in different textures. Green #1 fabrics will be mixed and matched among the blocks as follows:
    Cut 50 squares 4½" x 4½" (Pies)
    Cut 50 sets of 5 rectangles 2½" x 3½" (Spires)
    Cut 50 sets of 6 rectangles 3" x 4" (Background Spires)

• **Green #2:** ⅓ yard (Cattail Stems)

• **Brown:** ⅛ yard (Cattail Tops)

• **Pinks, Purples, or Scraps:** Total of 1½ yards (Flowers)

• **Purple:** ¼ yard (Frog)

• **Backing and matching hanging sleeve:** 4¼ yards
    2 cuts of 40" x 72" each

• **Batting:** 72" x 72"

• **Binding:** ½ yard

Sewing

Make:
• 50 New York Beauty blocks with Regular Arcs.

Following the assembly diagram, lay out the blocks. Move the blocks around until you have a visually pleasing arrangement among New York Beauty and Alternate blocks. Stitch the blocks together.

Adding the Appliqué

Since this book's focus is not on appliqué, I'll only give you some general hints. Please check the resource section for recommended in-depth instruction on appliqué.

My preferred method of appliqué is fusing the pieces down with a repositionable fusible web and then stitching the pieces down during the quilting process in what is referred to as raw-edge appliqué. You are most welcome to use your favorite appliqué method.

There are many fusible web products on the market. Please read the instructions for the product that you purchase. Generally, the fusible product has two sides; one is a smooth paper side, the other is the nubby web side.

Place the fusible web nubby side against the pattern piece and trace the pattern shape on the paper side. Cut these shapes out loosely leaving about ¼" to ½" around each piece.

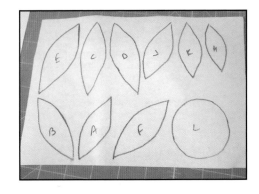

Place the shapes nubby side down on the wrong side of the chosen fabric and press with an iron. Do not over press, as you could melt the fusible too much and you will not have enough sticky stuff for the next process.

Cut each piece out on the drawn line. Do not remove the paper until you are ready to use the piece.

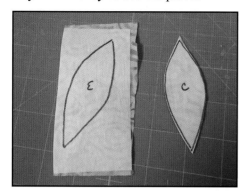

For an appliqué piece that has many components, place a Teflon® pressing sheet over the appliqué pattern. The translucent sheet allows me to see where the pieces go. Once I am satisfied with the positioning of the pieces, I very lightly fuse them together with a hot dry iron to create one appliqué piece.

Place the background petals first, following the pattern, and then "eyeball" the placement of the other pieces. The waterlilies don't have to all look exactly the same.

Take this assembled piece to your quilt and place it where you choose. Once you are happy with the final arrangement, fuse the appliqué to your quilt with a hot dry iron.

To make the cattails (that is what we called them when we were growing up on Staten Island), fuse several pieces of green fabric to a piece of fusible web about 6" to 8" wide and 12" to 18" long. Using your rotary cutter, freehand cut a variety of sizes and lengths of stems.

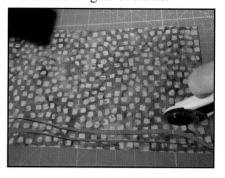

Be careful not to cut the green stem pieces too small—remember you have to eventually quilt them.

After removing the paper backing from the stems, you will be able to shape the curve of the stem easily, as they are cut on the bias. Make some stems long, some short, and use a variety of fabrics and shades of green. Shape some bending to the left, some to the right. Have fun.

I quilt and stitch down the appliqué at the same time, which is referred to as raw-edge appliqué.

Fuse the stems down and then add the cattail tops. Fuse the water lilies to the lily pads.

Quilt, bind, label, and enjoy!

Quilting hint: This piece was quilted on a longarm machine and a domestic machine. Sarah meandered the background first. The author quilted the New York Beauty blocks and then heavily raw-edge quilted the stems and flowers.

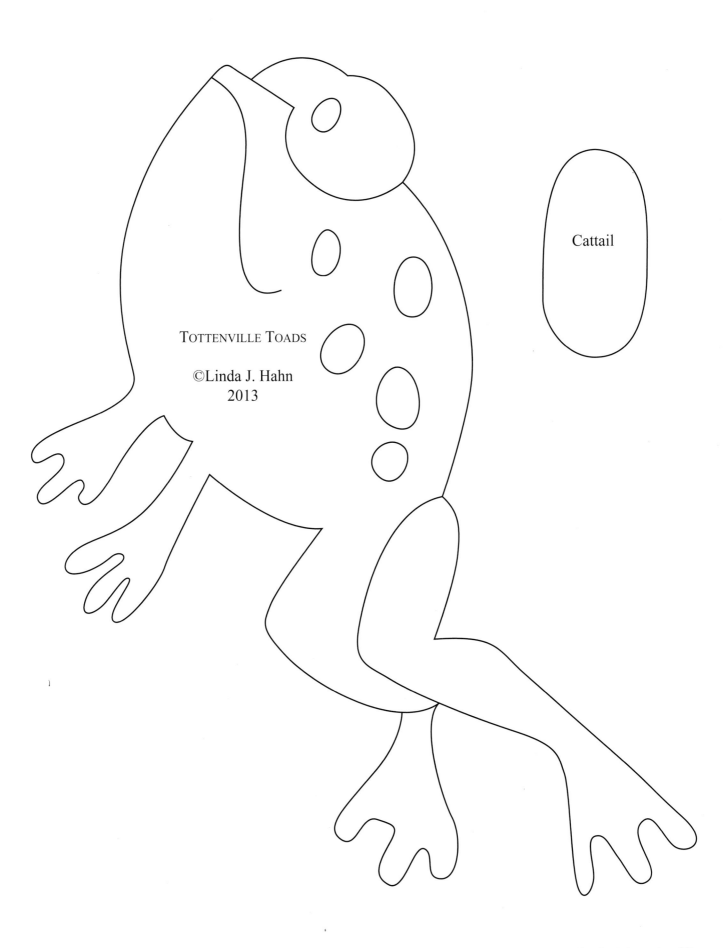

Cattail

Tottenville Toads

©Linda J. Hahn
2013

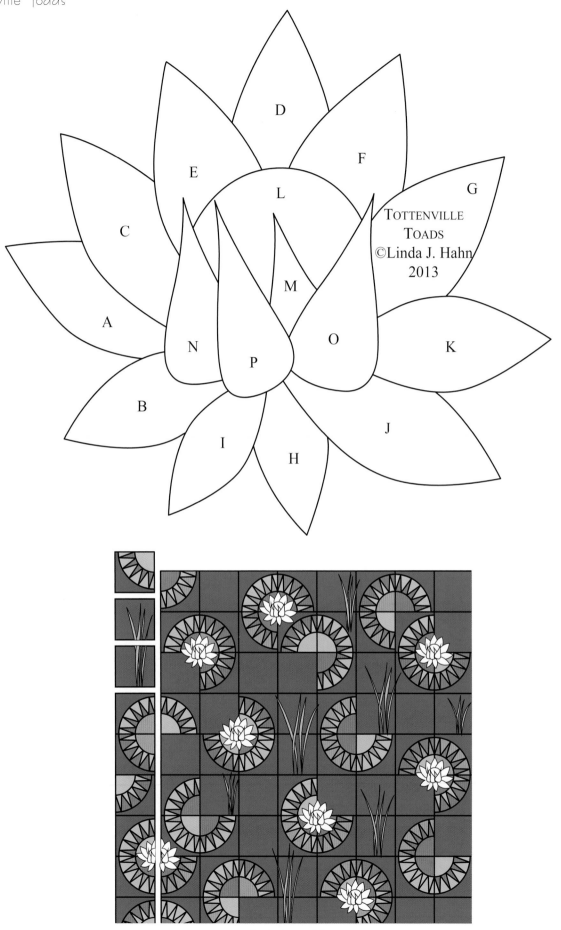

Tottenville
Toads
©Linda J. Hahn
2013

Quilt Assembly

Lily Pad
TOTTENVILLE TOADS

©Linda J. Hahn
2013

Niagara Nights 2, 45" x 45". Made by Stacey L. D. Moss, Freehold, New Jersey. Quilted by Sarah L. Hahn.

Niagara

NIGHTS 2

Beautiful colors appear under Niagara Falls in the evening and light up the sky. Stacey used fabrics from Clothworks™ Textiles to light up her quilt.

Blocks You Will Make

- 4 Burst blocks (page 20)
- Flower blocks with Split Spires (page 17)
- Beauty-in-a-Square blocks with Regular Arcs (page 27)
- 1 Square-in-a-Square block (page 25)
- 12 Beauty-in-the-Cabin blocks with Regular Arcs (page 17)

Foundations You Will Need

- 16 Regular Arcs (template on page 93). Use EQ paper. 2 per page = 8 pages.
- 4 Split Spires (template on page 94). Use EQ paper. 2 per page = 2 pages.
- 1 Square-in-a-Square block (template on page 26). Use any foundation paper. 1 page.
- 16 Burst blocks (template on page 22). Use EQ paper. 2 per page, need 4 per block = 32 pages.
- 4 Flower blocks (template on page 19). Use any foundation paper. 1 set per block per page = 4 pages.

Fabrics

- **Black:** 2 yards
  Cut 6 squares 6½" x 6½" in half on the diagonal (Square-in-a-Square/Beauty-in-a-Square)
  Cut 4 squares 8" x 8" (Flower blocks)
  Cut 60 rectangles 2½" x 3½" (Regular Arc Spires)
  Cut 16 rectangles 3" x 3½" (Burst blocks)
  Cut 16 squares 5" x 5" in half on the diagonal (Burst blocks)
  Cut 32 rectangles 2" x 5" (Burst blocks)
  Cut 4 rectangles 3½" x 7" (Flower blocks)
  Cut 4 rectangles 3½" x 10" (Flower blocks)
  Cut 12 rectangles 1¾" x 8" (Beauty-in-the-Cabins)
  Cut 12 rectangles 1¾" x 9" (Beauty-in-the-Cabins)

- **Magenta:** 1 yard
  Cut 12 rectangles 1¾" x 6½" (Beauty-in-the-Cabins)
  Cut 12 rectangles 1¾" x 8" (Beauty-in-the-Cabins)
  Cut 64 rectangles 2" x 4½" (Burst Spires)

- **Bright Pink:** ⅓ yard
  Cut 4 squares 6½" x 6½" in half on the diagonal (Beauty-in-a-Square blocks)

  Cut 12 rectangles 1½" x 3½" (Split Spire Arcs)

- **Cheddar:** 1¼ yards
  Cut 12 squares 4½" x 4½" (Pies)

- **Bright Orange:** ¼ yard
  Cut 8 squares 5" x 5" in half on the diagonal (Burst blocks)
  Cut 1 square 3½" x 3½" (Square-in-a-Square block)
  Cut 12 rectangles 1½" x 3½" (Split Spire Arcs)

- **Purple #1:** ¾ yard
  Cut 12 squares 8" x 8" (Backgrounds)
  Cut 4 squares 4½" x 4½" (Pies cut from Background scraps)
  Cut 2 squares 6½" x 6½" in half on the diagonal (Square-in-a-Square Round 3)

- **Purple #2:** ¼ yard
  Cut 4 squares 8" x 8" (Cut 4 squares 4½" x 4½" for Pies after you cut these Background pieces)

- **Light blue:** ¼ yard
  Cut 24 rectangles 3" x 4" (Background Spires)

- **Bright red print:** ½ yard
  Cut 2 squares 5" x 5" in half on the diagonal (Square-in-a-Square Round 2)
  Cut 72 rectangles 3" x 4" (Backgrounds)

- **Green #1:** ¼ yard
  Cut 20 rectangles 2½" x 3½" (Spires)

- **Green #2:** ½ yard
  Cut 4 squares 5" x 5" in half on the diagonal (Flower Stems)
  Cut 4 rectangles 3" x 7" (Flower Stems)
  Cut 4 rectangles 2" x 4" (Flower Stems)

- **Backing and matching hanging sleeve:** 3⅛ yards
  2 cuts of 40" x 53" each, pieced vertically

- **Batting:** 53" x 53"

- **Binding:** ½ yard Black

Sewing

Make:

- 4 Burst blocks.
- 4 Flower blocks.
- 4 Beauty-in-a-Square blocks.
- 1 Square-in-a-Square block.
- 12 Beauty-in-the-Cabin blocks.

Follow the assembly diagram to construct the top.

When you are laying out the blocks for this quilt, make sure you check and double check the orientation of the Flower blocks to make sure that the point of the stem is aimed toward the center.

Quilt, label, bind, and admire!

Quilt Assembly

Quilting Design

NIAGARA NIGHTS, 45" x 45". Made by the author.

MIDTOWN MADNESS, 52" x 52". Made by Debbie Welch, Bayville, New Jersey. Quilted by the author.

Midtown

MADNESS

This is a companion piece to Niagara Nights 2 (page 42). We mixed and matched the blocks and then set them on the diagonal with pieced side triangles for a new look.

Blocks You Will Make

- 12 New York Beauty blocks with Regular Arc (page 11)
- 4 Split Spires (page 94)
- 4 Burst blocks (page 20)
- 4 Square-in-a-Square blocks (page 25)
- 4 Flower blocks (page 17)
- Pieced Side Triangles (page 48)

Foundations You Will Need

- 12 New York Beauty blocks with Regular Arcs (template on page 93). Use EQ paper. 2 per page = 6 pages.
- 4 Split Spires (template on page 94). Use EQ paper. 2 per page = 2 pages.
- 16 Burst blocks (template on page 22). Use EQ paper. 2 per page, 4 per block = 32 pages.
- 4 Square-in-a-Square blocks (template on page 26). Use any foundation paper. 1 per page = 4 pages.
- 4 Flower blocks (template on page 19). Use any foundation paper. 1 per page = 4 pages.

Fabrics

- **Black:** 1½ yards
    Cut 16 rectangles 3" x 3½" (Burst blocks)
    Cut 16 squares 4½" x 4½" in half on the diagonal (Burst blocks)
    Cut 16 rectangles 2" x 5" (Burst blocks)
    Cut 6 rectangles 1¾" x 1¾" x 8" (Beauty-in-the-Cabin blocks)
    Cut 6 rectangles 1¾" x 9" (Beauty-in-the-Cabin blocks)
    Cut 4 rectangles 3½" x 7" (Flower blocks)
    Cut 4 rectangles 3½" x 9" (Flower blocks)
    Cut 16 squares 7" x 7" in half on the diagonal (Square-in-a-Square/Beauty-in-a-Square)
    Cut 16 squares 3½" x 3½" in half on the diagonal (Pieced Side Triangles)
    Cut 8 squares 5" x 5" in half on the diagonal (Pieced Side Triangles)

- **Solid pink:** ½ yard (Burst blocks)
    Cut 64 rectangles 2" x 4½"

- **Orange print:** ¼ yard (Burst blocks)
    Cut 8 squares 5" x 5" in half on the diagonal

- **Pink print:** ¼ yard
    Cut 8 rectangles 1¾" x 8" (Beauty-in-the-Cabins)
    Cut 8 rectangles 1¾" x 9" (Beauty-in-the-Cabins)
    Cut 8 squares 4" x 4" in half on the diagonal (Square-in-a-Square blocks)
    Cut 12 rectangles 1½" x 4" (Split Spires)

- **Green/yellow print:** ¼ yard
    Cut 8 squares 4½" x 4½" (New York Beauty blocks)
    Cut 4 squares 5" x 5" in half on the diagonal (Flower blocks)
    Cut 4 squares 3½" x 3½" (Square-in-a-Square blocks)

- **Lime green:** ⅛ yard (Split Spires)
    Cut 16 rectangles 3" x 4"

- **Green print:** ⅛ yard (New York Beauty blocks)
    Cut 40 rectangles 2½" x 3½"

- **Dark orange:** ⅛ yard (New York Beauty blocks)
    Cut 24 rectangles 3" x 4"

- **Blue/green print:** ⅛ yard (New York Beauty blocks)
    Cut 48 rectangles 3" x 4"

- **Blue print:** ⅛ yard (Flower blocks)
    Cut 4 rectangles 2½" x 4½"
    Cut 4 rectangles 3" x 7½"

- **Light purple:** ⅛ yard (or scraps) (Split Spires)
    Cut 12 rectangles 1½" x 4"

- **Dark purple**: 1 yard
    Cut 16 rectangles 3½" x 6½" (Pieced Side Triangles)
    Cut 8 squares 8"x 8" (New York Beauty blocks)
    Cut 4 squares 4½" x 4½" (Split Spires)
    Cut 8 squares 5" x 5" in half on the diagonal (Square-in-a-Square blocks)

- **Yellow:** ⅛ yard (New York Beauty blocks)
  Cut 4 squares 4½" x 4½"

- **Red:** ⅛ yard (New York Beauty blocks)
  Cut 20 rectangles 2½" x 3½"

- **Backing and matching hanging sleeve**: 3½ yards
  2 cuts of 40" x 60" each, pieced vertically

- **Batting:** 60" x 60"

- **Binding:** ½ yard Pink batik

Sewing

Make:
- 12 New York Beauty blocks.
- 4 Split Spires.
- 4 Burst blocks.
- 4 Square-in-a-Square blocks.
- 4 Flower blocks.
- 16 Pieced Side Triangles.

Follow the assembly diagram and lay out the blocks and
  Pieced Side Triangles.

Quilt, bind, label, and enjoy!

Pieced Side Triangles (12" x 8½" x 8½" finished)

Add a small triangle to each of the short sides of a 3½" x
6½" rectangle.

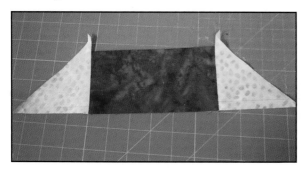

Add the large triangle to the top of the unit that you just
stitched together.

Trim this unit, making sure there is ¼" at the intersections
so you don't cut off the points.

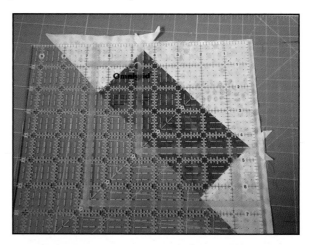

Quilting Assembly

Quilting Design

SARATOGA SALSA, 68" x 68". Made by the author. Quilted by Sarah L. Hahn.

Saratoga

SALSA

This collection of bright batiks from Timeless Treasures screams PARRTTAAYYY! This particular quilt is my husband's favorite. It is one of three quilts that use similar blocks, CONEY ISLAND CARNIVAL, page 54, and NEW DORP NEUTRALS, page 58, being the others. See how merely changing the colors and moving the blocks around give the quilts different, distinctive looks.

Blocks You Will Make
- 16 Flower blocks with Split Spire Arcs (page 17)
- 12 Swirl blocks (page 23)
- 36 Beauty-in-the-Cabin blocks with Regular Arcs (page 17)

Foundations You Will Use
- 36 Regular Arcs (template on page 93). Use EQ paper. 2 per page = 18 pages.
- 16 Split Spires (template on page 94). Use EQ paper. 2 per page = 8 pages.
- 48 Swirl blocks (template on page 24). Use EQ paper. Need 4 per block, 2 per page = 96 pages.
- 16 Flower blocks (template on page 19). Use tear-away paper. 1 per page = 16 pages.

Fabrics
- **Red print:** 1 yard (Beauty-in-the-Cabin blocks)
  Cut 32 rectangles 1¾" x 8"
  Cut 32 rectangles 1¾" x 9"

- **Orange/red print:** 1 yard (Beauty-in-the-Cabin blocks)
  Cut 32 rectangles 1¾" x 6½"
  Cut 32 rectangles 1¾" x 8"

- **Purple:** 2 yards
  Cut 36 squares 8" x 8" (Beauty-in-the-Cabin blocks)
  Cut 7 strips 2½" x width of fabric (Binding)

- **Dark orange:** 1¼ yards (Regular Arc Background Spires)
  Cut 216 rectangles 3" x 4"

- **Yellow:** 1 yard (Regular Arc Spires)
  Cut 180 rectangles 2½" x 3½"

- **Pink:** 1½ yards
  Cut 36 squares 4½" x 4½" (Regular Pies)
  Cut 16 squares 5" x 5" cut in half on the diagonal (Flower Leaves)
  Cut 16 rectangles 3" x 7½" (Flower Leaves)
  Cut 16 rectangles 2½" x 4½" (Flower Leaves)

- **Dark magenta:** 1 yard
  Cut 16 squares 8" x 8" (Split Spire Backgrounds)
  Cut 24 squares 2½" x 2½" (Center Swirls. Cut these small squares from what is left over after you use the template to cut out the Flower Backgrounds.)

- **Yellow print:** 1½ yards
  Cut 48 rectangles 3" x 4" (Split Spire Background Spires)
  Cut 66 rectangles 3" x 6" (Outer Swirls)

- **Dark pink print:** ¾ yard
  Cut 16 squares 4½" x 4½" (Split Spire Pies)
  Cut 48 rectangles 1½" x 3½" (Split Spires)

- **Orange:** 1 yard
  Cut 48 rectangles 1½" x 3½" (Split Spire Arcs)
  Cut 16 rectangles 3½" x 7" (Flowers)
  Cut 16 rectangles 3½" x 9" (Flowers)

- **Pink print:** 1 yard (Swirl blocks)
  Cut 48 rectangles 3" x 6"

- **Red/orange print:** 1 yard (Swirl blocks)
  Cut 48 rectangles 2½" x 6½"

- **Backing and matching hanging sleeve:** 4½ yards
  2 cuts of 40" x 76" each, pieced vertically

- **Batting:** 76" x 76"

- **Binding:** ½ yard included in Purple yardage

Sewing

Make:

- 16 Flower blocks with Split Spire Arcs.
- 12 Swirl blocks.
- 36 Beauty-in-the-Cabin blocks with Regular Arcs.

Follow the assembly diagram to construct the top.

When you are laying out the blocks for this quilt, check and double check the orientation of the Flower blocks to make sure that the point of the stem is pointing towards the center.

Quilt, label, bind, and admire!

Quilt Assembly

Quilting Design

Quilt Detail

CONEY ISLAND CARNIVAL, 60" x 60". Made by the author. Quilted by Sarah L. Hahn.

Coney Island

CARNIVAL

Happy and fun is the flavor of this quilt. Cotton candy-colored batiks are from the Hoffman California 1895 batik collection. This is one of three quilts that demonstrate how merely changing the fabric/color and mixing the blocks up can completely change the feeling or essence of the quilt. The other two are SARATOGA SALSA (page 50) and NEW DORP NEUTRALS (page 58).

Blocks You Will Make
- 32 New York Beauty blocks with Regular Arcs (page 11)
  - 16 of these are for Beauty-in-the-Cabin blocks (page 17)
  - 8 of these are for Beauty-in-a-Square blocks (page 27)
  - 8 of these are for Flower blocks (page 17)
- 5 Square-in-a-Square blocks (page 25)
- 12 Burst blocks (page 20)

Foundations You Will Use
- 5 Square-in-a-Square blocks (template on page 26). Use any foundation paper. 1 per page = 5 pages.
- 96 Burst blocks (template on page 22). Use EQ paper. 2 per page, need 4 per block = 48 pages.
- 8 Flower blocks (template on page 19). Use any foundation paper. 1 set per block per page = 8 pages.
- 32 Regular Arcs (template on page 93). Use EQ paper. 2 per page = 16 pages.93

Fabrics
- **Yellow:** 1¼ yards (Spires)
  Cut 160 rectangles 2½" x 3½"

- **Orange:** 1¾ yards (Background Spires)
  Cut 192 rectangles 3" x 4"

- **Bright Pink:** 1½ yards (Background)
  Cut 32 squares 8"x 8"

- **Magenta:** 1½ yards (Burst Spires)
  Cut 192 rectangles 2" x 4½"

- **Red:** ⅜ yard (Square-in-a-Square blocks)
  Cut 10 squares 5" x 5" cut in half on the diagonal

- **Blue #1:** 1¾ yards (Burst Background)
  Cut 48 rectangles 3" x 3½"
  Cut 48 squares 4½" x 4½" in half on the diagonal
  Cut 48 rectangles 2" x 5"

- **Blue #2:** ¼ yard (Flower blocks)
  Cut 8 rectangles 3" x 7"
  Cut 8 rectangles 3" x 9"

- **Blue #3:** ½ yard (Pies)
  Cut 32 squares 4½" x 4½"

- **Green:** ½ yard (Flower blocks)
  Cut 8 squares 5" x 5" in half on the diagonal
  Cut 8 rectangles 3" x 7½"
  Cut 8 rectangles 2 ¼" x 4½"

- **Pink #1:** ⅛ yard (Square-in-a-Square blocks)
  Cut 5 squares 3½" x 3½"

- **Pink #2:** 1 yard (Beauty-in-the-Cabin blocks)
  Cut 32 rectangles 1¾" x 6½"
  Cut 32 rectangles 1¾" x 8"

- **Purple #1:** ⅛ yard (Square-in-a-Square blocks)
  Cut 10 squares 4" x 4" in half on the diagonal

- **Purple #2:** ½ yard (Square-in-a-Square blocks)
  Cut 10 squares 6½" x 6½" in half on the diagonal

- **Purple #3:** 1 yard (Beauty-in-the-Cabin blocks)
  Cut 32 rectangles 1¾" x 8"
  Cut 32 rectangles 1¾" x 9"

- **Backing and matching hanging sleeve:** 4 yards
  2 cuts of 40" x 68" each, pieced vertically

- **Batting:** 68" x 68"

- **Binding:** ½ yard

Sewing

Make:

- 16 Beauty-in-the-Cabin blocks.

- 8 Beauty-in-the-Square blocks.

- 8 Flower blocks.

- 5 Square-in-a-Square blocks.

- 2 Burst blocks.

Follow the assembly diagram to create the top.

Quilt, bind, label, and enjoy!

Quilt Assembly

Quilting Design

Quilt Detail

New Dorp Neutrals, 68" x 68". Made and quilted by the author.

New Dorp

NEUTRALS

I was born on Staten Island and attended New Dorp High School. I wanted to include a quilt to commemorate my alma mater. "Dorp" is Dutch for "village." The sample quilt was quilted in a Featheration pantograph pattern.

Blocks You Will Make

- 36 Beauty-in-the-Cabin blocks with Regular Arcs (page 17)
- 4 Swirl blocks (page 23)
- 12 Burst blocks (page 20)
- 12 Flower blocks with Split Spire Arcs (page 17)

Foundations You Will Use

- 36 Regular Arcs (template on page 93). Use EQ paper. 2 per page = 18 pages.
- 16 Swirl blocks (template on page 24). Use EQ paper 2 per page = 8 pages.
- 48 Burst blocks (template on page 22). Use any foundation paper. 2 per page, 4 needed per block = 24 pages.
- 12 Flower blocks (templates on page 19). Use any foundation paper. I set per page = 12 pages.
- 8 Split Spires (template on page 94). Use EQ paper. 2 per page = 4 pages.

Fabrics

- **Dark grey:** 2 yards
  Cut 36 rectangles 1¾" x 8" (Beauty-in-the-Cabin blocks)
  Cut 36 rectangles 1¾" x 9" (Beauty-in-the-Cabin blocks)
  Cut 8 squares 8" x 8" (Split Spire Backgrounds)

- **Green:**
  Cut 36 rectangles 1¾" x 6½" (Swirl blocks)
  Cut 36 rectangles 1¾" x 8" (Beauty-in-the-Cabin blocks)

- **Light yellow:** 1 yard (Beauty-in-the-Cabin blocks)
  Cut 36 squares 8" x 8"

- **Dark orange:** 1¼ yards (Regular Arc Background Spires)
  Cut 216 rectangles 3" x 4"

- **Dusty Pink:** 1¼ yards (Regular Arc Spires and Split Spire Pies)
  Cut 180 rectangles 2½" x 3½"
  Cut 36 squares 4½" x 4½"

- **Light grey #1:** ½ yard (Pies)
  Cut 36 squares 4½" x 4½"

- **Light grey #2:** 1½ yards (Burst Backgrounds)
  Cut 48 rectangles 3" x 3½"
  Cut 48 squares 4½" x 4½" in half on the diagonal
  Cut 48 rectangles 2" x 5"

- **Light grey #3:** ¼ yard (Pies)
  Cut 36 squares 4½" x 4½"

- **Black:** 2 yards
  Cut 192 rectangles 2" x 4½" (Burst Spires)
  Cut 16 squares 2½" x 2½" in half on the diagonal (Swirl blocks)
  Cut 6 strips 2½" x width of fabric (Binding)

- **Medium grey:** ¾ yard (Flower blocks)
  Cut 12 rectangles 3½" x 7"
  Cut 12 rectangles 3½" x 9"

- **Dark green:** ½ yard (Flower blocks)
  Cut 12 squares 5" x 5" in half on the diagonal
  Cut 12 rectangles 3½" x 7"
  Cut 12 rectangles 2½" x 4½"

- **Medium brown:** ⅝ yard
  Cut 16 rectangles 3" x 6" (Swirl blocks)
  Cut 25 squares 5" x 5" in half on the diagonal (Burst Centers)

- **Gold:** ¾ yard
  Cut 36 rectangles 3" x 4" (Split Spire Backgrounds)
  Cut 16 rectangles 3" x 4" (Swirl blocks)

- **Backing and matching hanging sleeve:** 4½ yards
  2 cuts of 40" x 76" each, pieced vertically

- **Batting:** 76" x 76"

- **Binding:** ½ yard included in Black yardage

Sewing

Make:

- 12 Flower blocks with Split Spire Arcs.
- 4 Swirl blocks.
- 12 Burst blocks.
- 36 Beauty-in-the-Cabin blocks with Regular Arcs.

When you are laying out the blocks for this quilt, make sure you check and double check the orientation of the Flower blocks so the stems point toward the center.

Quilt, bind, label, and admire.

Quilt Assembly

Quilting Design

Quilt Detail

POUGHKEEPSIE PURPLE, 51" x 51". Made by Nancy Rock, Edison, New Jersey. Quilted by Sarah L. Hahn.

Poughkeepsie

PURPLE

This quilt brings Beauty-in-a-Square out into the borders.

Blocks You Will Make
- 4 Square-in-a-Square blocks (page 25)
- 8 Burst blocks (page 20)
- 8 Flower blocks (page 17)
- 16 Beauty-in-a-Square blocks (page 27)

Foundations You Will Use
- 4 Square-in-a-Square blocks (template on page 26). Use any foundation paper. 1 per page = 4 pages.
- 16 Burst blocks (template on page 22). Use EQ paper. 2 per page, need 4 per block = 32 pages.
- 20 Regular Arcs (template on page 93). Use EQ paper. 2 per page = 10 pages.
- 4 Split Spire Arcs (template on page 94). Use EQ paper. 2 per page = 2 pages.
- 8 Flower blocks (template on page 19). Use any foundation paper. 1 set per page = 8 pages.

Fabrics
- **Medium green:** ½ yard (Beauty-in-a-Square blocks)
  Cut 16 squares 6½" x 6½"

- **Light green:** ½ yard (Corner Flowers/ Square-in-a-Square blocks)
  Cut 4 squares 5" x 5" in half on the diagonal
  Cut 4 rectangles 3" x 7½"
  Cut 4 rectangles 2½" x 4½"

- **Olive green:** ¼ yard (Center Flowers)
  Cut 4 squares 5" x 5" in half on the diagonal
  Cut 4 rectangles 3" x 7½"
  Cut 4 rectangles 2½" x 4½"

- **Dark purple:** 1 yard (Square-in-a-Squares/Backgrounds)
  Cut 8 squares 6½" x 6½" in half on the diagonal
  Cut 20 squares 8" x 8"

- **Medium purple #1:** ½ yard (Beauty-in-a-Square blocks)
  Cut 16 squares 6½" x 6½"

- **Medium purple #2:** ½ yard (Pies)
  Cut 20 squares 4½" x 4½"

- **Blue purple:** ½ yard (Burst Centers)
  Cut 16 squares 5" x 5" in half on the diagonal

- **Light blue:** ½ yard (Pies/Corner Flower Backgrounds)
  Cut squares 4½" x 4½"
  Cut 4 rectangles 3" x 7½"
  Cut 4 rectangles 3" x 9½"

- **Medium blue:** 1½ yards (Burst Backgrounds)
  Cut 32 rectangles 3" x 3½"
  Cut 32 rectangles 4½" x 4½" in half on the diagonal
  Cut 32 rectangles 2" x 5"

- **Dark blue:** ¼ yard (Center Flower Backgrounds)
  Cut 4 rectangles 3" x 7½"
  Cut 4 rectangles 3" x 9½"

- **Light teal:** 1½ yards (Background Spires)
  Cut 100 rectangles 2½" x 3½"
  Cut 16 rectangles 3½" x 4"

- **Dark teal:** ¾ yard (Spires/Square-in-a-Square blocks)
  Cut 8 squares 5" x 5" in half on the diagonal
  Cut 80 rectangles 2½" x 3½"

- **Red:** ⅛ yard (Spires)
  Cut 12 rectangles 1½" x 3½"
  Cut 24 rectangles 2½" x 3½"

- **Orange:** ⅛ yard (Spires)
  Cut 12 rectangles 1½" x 3½"
  Cut 8 rectangles 2½" x 3½"

- **Medium Pink:** ½ yard (Burst Spires)
  Cut 128 rectangles 2" x 4½"

- **Hot Pink:** ¼ yard (Backgrounds/Square-in-a-Squares)
  Cut 8 squares 4" x 4" in half on the diagonal
  Cut 4 squares 8" x 8"

- **Backing:** 3½ yards
  2 cuts of 40" x 59" each, pieced vertically

- **Batting:** 59" x 59"

- **Binding:** ½ yard

Sewing

Make:

- 4 Square-in-a-Square blocks.
- 8 Burst blocks.
- 8 Flower blocks.
- 16 Beauty-in-a-Square blocks.

Following the assembly diagram, lay out your blocks and assemble the quilt.

Quilt, bind, label, and enjoy!

Quilt Assembly

Quilting Design

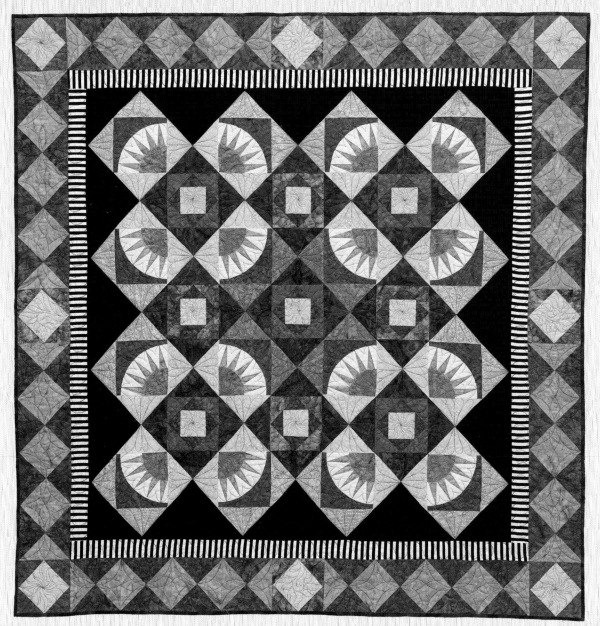

Moonlight Over Montauk, 66" x 66". Made by Janet Byard, Lawrenceville, New Jersey. Quilted by Sarah L. Hahn.

Moonlight
Over
MONTAUK

Beautiful tone-on-tone and small print fabrics from Timeless Treasures sparkle just like moonlight shining over Montauk Bay. Color placement creates the secondary Ohio Star effect.

Blocks You Will Make

- 16 Beauty-in-a-Square blocks (page 27)
- 9 Square-in-a-Square blocks (page 68)

Foundations You Will Use

- 16 Regular Arcs (template on page 93). Use EQ paper. 2 per page = 8 pages.
- 9 Square-in-a-Square blocks (template on page 26). Use any foundation paper. 1 per page = 9 pages.

Fabrics

- **Stripe**: 1 yard (Inner Border)
  Cut 2 strips 2½" x 48½"
  Cut 2 strips 2½" x 52½"

- **Black**: ¾ yard (Setting Triangles)
  Cut 5 squares 10½" x 10½" in half on the diagonal

- **Lime green**: ¾ yard
  Cut 4 squares 4½" x 4½" (Outer Border)
  Cut 16 squares 7" x 7" in half on the diagonal
     (Beauty-in-the-Square blocks)
  Cut 9 squares 3½" x 3½"
     (Square-in-a-Square blocks)

- **Medium green**: ¼ yard
  Cut 8 squares 4" x 4" in half on the diagonal
     (Outer Border)
  Cut 8 squares 3½" x 3½"
     (Square-in-a-Square blocks)

- **Light teal**: 1 yard (Background Spires)
  Cut 96 rectangles 3" x 4"

- **Purple/blue**: ½ yard
  Cut 16 squares 4½" x 4½" (Pies)
  Cut 4 squares 7" x 7" in half on the diagonal
     (Beauty-in-the-Square blocks)

- **Purple**: ¾ yard (Backgrounds)
  Cut 16 squares 8" x 8"

- **Medium purple**: ⅝ yard (Outer Border)
  Cut 16 squares 7½" x 7½" in half on the diagonal

- **Dark purple**: ⅓ yard (Square-in-a-Square blocks)
  Cut 9 squares 6½" x 6½" in half on the diagonal

- **Purpley pink**: ¼ yard (Square-in-a-Square blocks)
  Cut 18 squares 4" x 4" in half on the diagonal

- **Medium teal**: 1½ yards
  Cut 80 rectangles 2½" x 3½" (Spires)
  Cut 16 squares 7½" x 7½" in half on the diagonal
     (Outer Border)

- **Light blue print**: ½ yard (Beauty-in-the-Square blocks)
  Cut 12 squares 7" x 7" in half on the diagonal

- **Bright blue**: ⅜ yard (Square-in-a-Square blocks)
  Cut 10 squares 5" x 5" in half on the diagonal

- **Backing and matching hanging sleeve**: 4½ yards
  2 cuts of 40" x 74" each, pieced vertically

- **Batting**: 74" x 74"

- **Binding**: ½ yard of a coordinating purple

Sewing

Make:

- 16 Beauty-in-the-Square blocks using the light blue print for the top triangles and the lime green for the bottom triangles.

- 5 Square-in-a-Square blocks using the bright blue fabric for Round 3.

- 4 Square-in-a-Square blocks using the green fabric for Round 3.

Moonlight Over Montauk

Assemble the top in diagonal rows.

See Adding Borders on page 8 to add the striped inner border. Heavy starching will help keep your stripes straight as you stitch them on.

Make 4 Square-in-a-Square blocks using lime green squares for the center and bright blue squares for the triangle pieces, using the Simple Method:

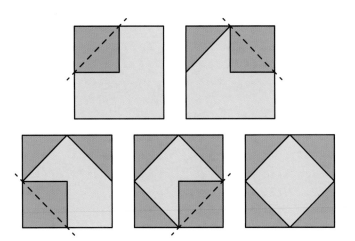

Repeat, making (4) Square-in-a-Square blocks using lime green squares for the center and medium green for the triangle pieces. Trim to 6½".

Using the Purple and medium Teal triangles, stitch 16 quarter-square triangles. After stitching together, trim blocks to 6½".

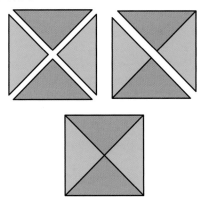

Referring to the photograph, lay out the quilt and assemble.

Quilt, bind, label, and enjoy!

Quilt Assembly

Quilting Design

BRIGHTON BEACH BAZAAR, 56½" x 56½". Designed and made by Helle-May Cheney, Flemington, New Jersey. Quilted by Sarah L. Hahn.

Brighton
Beach
BAZAAR

The use of Split Pies and Split Backgrounds with a few Solid Arcs gives this quilt added dimension and a distinctive look. The colors were inspired by Russian nesting dolls (Matryoshka). Brighton Beach is home to a large Russian community.

Blocks You Will Make

- 32 New York Beauty blocks with Regular Arcs (page 11)
- 32 Alternate blocks (page 72)

Foundations You Will Use

- 32 Regular Arcs (template on page 93). Use EQ paper. 2 per page = 16 pages.
- 32 Solid Arcs (template on page 75).
- 64 Split Backgrounds (template on page 74). 3 per page = 22 pages.

Fabrics

- **Black small print:** 2 yards
  - Cut 32 squares 4½" x 4½" (Pies in New York Beauty blocks)
  - Cut 16 rectangles 3½" x 4" (Split Pies)
  - Cut 32 rectangles 3" x 7" (Split Backgrounds)
  - Cut 2 strips 3½" x 48½" from length of fabric (Outer Border)
  - Cut 2 strips 3½" x 56½" from length of fabric (Outer Border)

- **Red:** 2 yards
  - Cut 6 strips 2½" x width of fabric (Binding)
  - Cut 16 squares 8½" x 8½" (Background)
  - Cut 32 rectangles 3½" x 4" (Split Pies) from leftover Background pieces
  - Cut 96 rectangles 3" x 4" (Background Spires)
  - Cut 80 rectangles 2½" x 3½" (Spires)

- **Blue:** ½ yard
  - Cut 16 squares 6½" x 6½" (Solid Arcs)

- **Yellow:** 2 yards
  - Cut 2 strips 1½" x 48½" (Inner Border)
  - Cut 2 strips 1½" x 50½" (Inner Border)
  - Cut 16 squares 8" x 8" (Background)
  - Cut 80 rectangles 2½" x 3½" (Spires)
  - Cut 96 rectangles 3" x 4" (Background Spires)
  - Cut 32 rectangles 3" x 7" (Split Backgrounds)

- **Backing and matching hanging sleeve:** 4 yards
  - 2 cuts of 40" x 65" each, pieced vertically

- **Batting:** 65" x 65"

- **Binding:** ½ yard included in Red yardage

Additional Information

This quilt features Split Backgrounds and Split Pie shapes. As you work with these split pieces, it's important to pay attention that the fabrics are on the correct side of the split or you'll be doing some ripping. (Ask me how I know that!)

Cut pieces right to the templates for this quilt.

Construction

Make:

- 16 New York Beauty blocks with Regular Arcs:
  - Red Background
  - Red Background Spires
  - Yellow Spires
  - Black Pie

- 16 New York Beauty blocks with Regular Arcs:
  - Yellow Background
  - Yellow Background Spires
  - Red Spires
  - Black Pie

32 Alternate blocks (page 72)

Following the quilt assembly diagram, lay out and assemble the quilt top. Add borders (page 73).

Quilt, bind, label, and enjoy!

Make Alternate Blocks

Editor's note: The sample quilt directions call for black fabric. Other colors are shown here for better viewing.

Stitch the 3½" x 4" rectangles together. Use the acrylic templates or make your own template of the Split Pie shape with a diagonal line down the center.

Place the Pie template on the right side of the stitched rectangles. Cut right to the template—do not leave any additional fabric around the template.

Cut 16 Pies with the black fabric on the right side of the split and 16 with the black fabric on the left side.

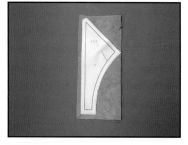

Make a template of the Split Background.

Place 16 black rectangles 3" x 7" wrong sides together with 16 of the yellow rectangles 3" x 7" with the BLACK ON TOP.

Cut out the Split Background fabric pieces to the template.

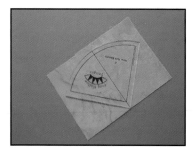

Repeat, putting the YELLOW RECTANGLES ON TOP wrong sides together with the black rectangles.

Hint: Cutting in this fashion makes sure that you are getting the fabric cut with the colors in the right orientation.

Stitch the pieces together on the short side. Press the seam open.

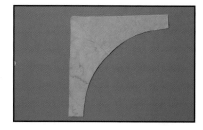

Make a template of the Solid Arc. Place on a 6½" fabric square, pin, and cut.

Fold the fabric Solid Arc in half and crease. Place the fabric Split Pie right sides together with the Solid Arc and drop a pin through the seam allowance of the Pie into the crease of the Solid Arc.

Line up the raw edges on the sides. Referring to the photo, insert the pins with the points facing up, and come back up approximately ⅛" to ¼" from the raw edges. This keeps the edges lined up and allows you to stitch exactly over the pin point.

Remove the pins and press towards the Solid Arc.

Repeat the pinning process for attaching the Split Background.

Press towards the Split Background. Trim the Alternate block to 6½" square.

Quilt Assembly

Quilting Design

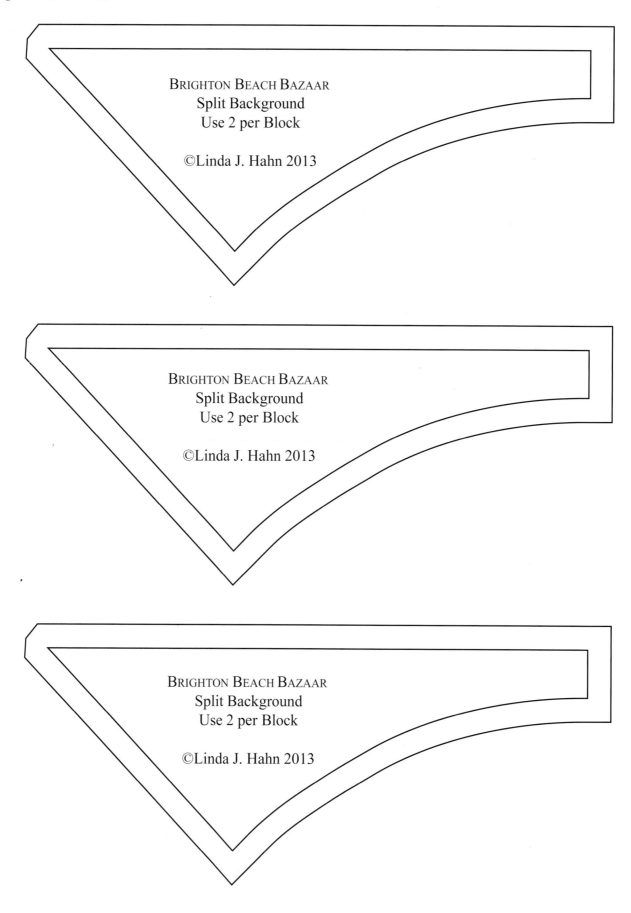

BRIGHTON BEACH BAZAAR
Split Background
Use 2 per Block

©Linda J. Hahn 2013

BRIGHTON BEACH BAZAAR
Split Background
Use 2 per Block

©Linda J. Hahn 2013

BRIGHTON BEACH BAZAAR
Split Background
Use 2 per Block

©Linda J. Hahn 2013

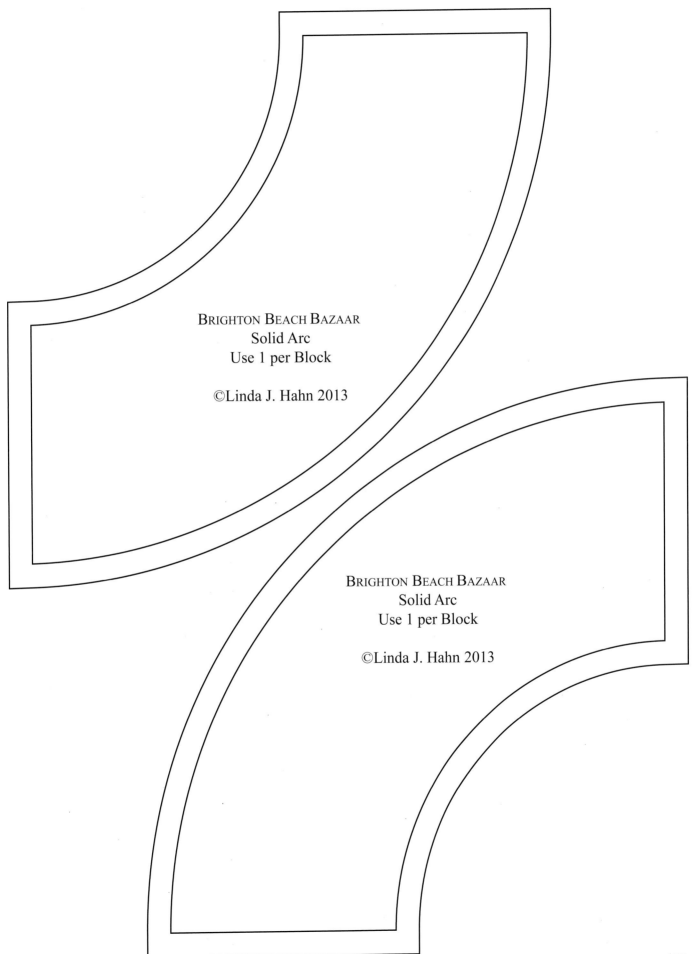

BRIGHTON BEACH BAZAAR
Solid Arc
Use 1 per Block

©Linda J. Hahn 2013

BRIGHTON BEACH BAZAAR
Solid Arc
Use 1 per Block

©Linda J. Hahn 2013

Buffalo Bubblegum, 48" x 48". Made by Rebecca Szabo, Howell, New Jersey. Quilted by Sarah L. Hahn.

Buffalo

BUBBLEGUM

These colors are right out of the bubblegum machine! The best part about making this stunner is that there are NO set-in seams! Choose fabrics that will hide seam lines for the best effect.

Blocks You Will Make
- 20 New York Beauty blocks with Regular Arcs (page 11)
- 36 Half-Square Triangles (page 77)

Foundations You Will Use
- 20 Regular Arcs (template on page 93). Use EQ paper. 2 per page = 10 pages.

Fabrics
- **Teal:** ¼ yard (Inner Star)
    Cut 2 squares 5" x 5"
    Cut 4 rectangles 2½" x 4½"
    Cut 2 squares 6½" x 6½" in half on the diagonal

- **Teal print:** ¼ yard (Inner Star)
    Cut 2 squares 5" x 5"
    Cut 4 rectangles 2½" x 4½"
    Cut 2 squares 6½" x 6½" in half on the diagonal

- **Purple:** ¼ yard (Pies)
    Cut 20 squares 4½" x 4½"

- **Orange:** ¾ yard (Spires)
    Cut 100 rectangles 2½" x 3½"

- **Small gold print:** 1¼ yards
    Cut 120 rectangles 3" x 4" (Background Spires)
    Cut 8 squares 8" x 8" (Backgrounds)

- **Pink print:** 1 yard (Outer Star)
    Cut 12 rectangles 2½" x 4½"
    Cut 12 squares 5" x 5"
    Cut 2 squares 6½" x 6½" in half on the diagonal

- **Magenta:** 1 yard (Outer Star/Binding)
    Cut 12 rectangles 2½" x 4½"
    Cut 12 squares 5" x 5"
    Cut 2 squares 6½" x 6½" in half on the diagonal

- **Yellow/green print:** 1½ yards
    Cut 12 squares 8" x 8" (Backgrounds)
    Cut 8 squares 5" x 5" (Backgrounds)
    Cut 2 strips 4" x 40½" (Border)
    Cut 2 strips 4" x 48½" (Border)

- **Backing and matching hanging sleeve:** 3⅓ yards
    2 cuts of 40" x 56" each, pieced vertically

- **Batting:** 56" x 56"

- **Binding:** ½ yard

Sewing
For this quilt, you will make and assemble the pieces into units, then into sections, and then stitch the sections together.

Half-Square Triangles (HST)
Place 2 squares right sides together and draw a diagonal line from corner to corner. Stitch ¼" away from each side of the drawn line. Cut apart on the drawn line and press to the darker of the 2 fabrics. Trim the HST to the indicated size.

To make 4½" UNfinished HSTs, use 5" squares in these combinations:
- 4 using teal and teal print (yields 8)
- 6 using magenta and pink (yields 12)
- 4 using magenta and green (yields 8)
- 2 using pink and green (yields 4)
- 2 using magenta and green (yields 4)

New York Beauty Blocks
Make:
- 12 New York Beauty blocks with a green background
- 8 New York Beauty blocks with a gold background

Once all of the units are assembled, you can begin making the sections.

Center Sections (Make 4)
Place a New York Beauty block with a gold background on a diagonal with the spires pointing up. Add a 6½"

triangle of teal print to the bottom left and a 6½" triangle of teal to the bottom right. Add a magenta triangle to the top left and a pink triangle to the top right.

Trim to 8½" following the trimming directions for the Beauty-in-the-Square on page 27.

Add a 2½" x 4½" magenta rectangle to the magenta side of a magenta/pink HST. Repeat with pink for the pink side.

Position a New York Beauty block with a green background with the Spires pointing up.

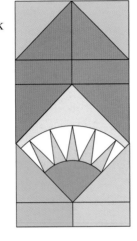

Following the diagram, stitch the magenta/pink unit to the top of the New York Beauty block.

Make 4 of these sections.

Side Sections (Make 4)
Stitch a 2½" x 4½" pink rectangle to the pink side of a magenta/pink HST.

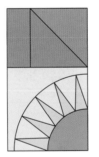

Following the diagram, stitch this unit to a New York Beauty block.

Stitch a 2½" x 4½" magenta rectangle to a magenta/pink HST. Add a magenta/pink HST to this unit.

Attach the new unit to the left side of the unit you made above, making sure that the colors are in the appropriate orientation.

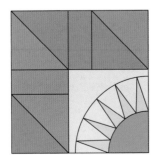

Stitch a 2½" x 4½" magenta rectangle to the bottom of a magenta/green HST.

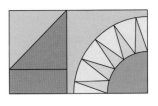

Place a New York Beauty block with a green background with spires up and to the left. Stitch the unit that you just made to the New York Beauty block.

Following the diagram, attach this unit to the unit you made in the previous step.

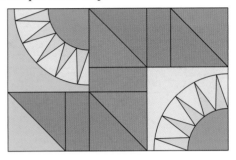

Stitch 2 New York Beauty blocks with a green background together into a Half Sun block.

Add a 2½" x 4½" pink rectangle to the magenta side of a magenta/green HST.

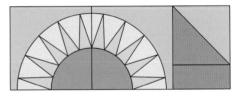

Stitch the HST unit to the right side of the Half Sun blocks.

Following the diagram, stitch the unit that you have just made to the unit that you made in the previous step.

Make 4 identical units.

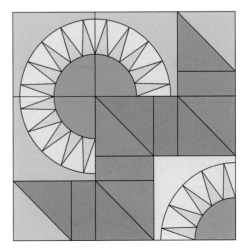

Following the diagram, stitch two corner units and a center unit together. Make 2.

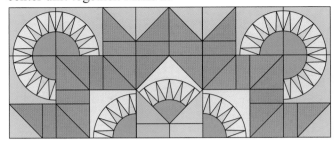

Stitch the teal HSTs into a pinwheel.

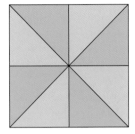

Add two center units to the Pinwheel unit.

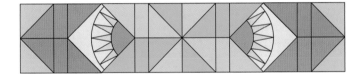

Stitch all three units together.

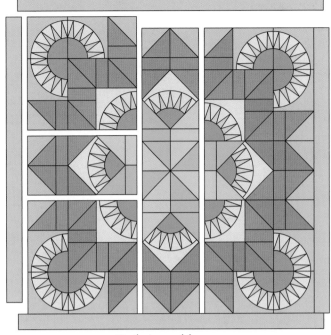

Quilt Assembly

Quilt, bind, label, and admire!

Quilting Design

Red Red Rochester, 57" x 57". Made by the author. Quilted by Sarah L. Hahn.

Red Red

ROCHESTER

If you do not want to make the Double Arc New York beauty block shown in the quilt, you can simply change the block to be one with a Regular Arc (page 93) or with a Split Spire (page 94).

I wanted a traditional flavor for this quilt, so I chose fabrics from the LaBelle collection from Northcott Silk, Inc. Use the photo to find similar fabrics at your local quilt shop.

Blocks or Units You Will Make
- 9 Corner Stars (page 82)
- 16 Double Arc New York Beauty blocks (page 82)
- 24 Spire Strip-Sets (page 12)

Foundations You Will Use
- 48 Spire Strips 2" x 6" (template on page 92). Use EQ paper. 4 per page = 12 pages.
- 16 Spire Arcs (template on pages 85–86). Use EQ paper. 3 per page = 6 pages.
- 9 Corner Stars (templates on page 87). Use any foundation paper. 1 star per page = 9 pages.

Fabrics
- **Large floral:** 2 yards
  Cut 2 strips 5½" x 44" (Outer Border sides)
  Cut 2 strips 5½" x 54½" (Outer Border top and bottom)
  Cut 8 rectangles 3½" x 12½" (Sashing)

- **Black print:** 1 yard
  Cut 2 strips 1½" x 42½" (Inner Border sides)
  Cut 2 strips 1½" x 45½" (Inner Border top and bottom)
  Cut 36 rectangles 2" x 4½" (Stars)

- **Light small print:** 3 yards (Backgrounds)
  Cut 16 squares 8" x 8"
  Cut 264 rectangles 2" x 3"
  Cut 36 squares 3½" x 3½" in half on the diagonal
  Cut 36 squares 2½" x 2½" in half on the diagonal

- **Red small print:** 1¾ yards
  Cut 240 rectangles 2" x 3" (Sashing Spires)
  Cut 36 rectangles 2" x 4½" (Star)

- **Multi-print:** ½ yard
  Cut 4 rectangles 3½" x 12½" (Sashing)
  Cut 16 squares 4½" x 4½" (Pies)

- **Blue:** ½ yard
  Cut 128 rectangles 1½" x 2½" (Spires)
  Cut 5 strips 2½" x width of fabric (Binding)

- **Green:** ¼ yard (Arcs)
  16 rectangles 3½" x 7"
  If you use the Regular Arc you do not need green fabric.

- **Light tone-on-tone:** 1 yard (Background Spires)
  44 rectangles 2" x 2½"

- **Backing and matching hanging sleeve:** 3⅞ yards
  2 cuts of 40" x 65" each, pieced vertically

- **Batting:** 65" x 65"

- **Binding:** ½ yard included in Blue yardage

Sewing
Spire Strip-Sets (Make 24)
Make a total of 48 Spire Strips using the red small print and the light small print fabrics.

Attach 2 Spire Strips together along the short side of the strips. Press the seam open. Repeat to make a total of 24 sets.

Stitch 1 set to the long side of a 3½" x 12½" Multi-print rectangle. Press towards the multi-print.

Attach the rest of the sets to the other side to create the sashing. Set these aside.

Corner Stars (Make 9)

Lay out your star foundation pieces in the correct orientation next to your sewing machine. You are doing this to make sure that you are stitching 4 of each orientation AND that you have your fabrics placed correctly.

Using the basic instructions for foundation piecing on pages 11–14, stitch each of the 8 Corner Star units, placing each unit back in its appropriate place beside your machine.

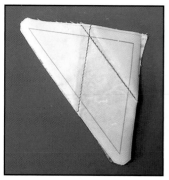 

Trim the pieced units to the outermost line and return them to their appropriate places in your layout.

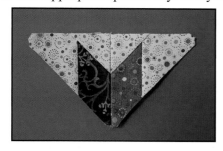

Begin stitching the units together in pairs. Press seam open.

Stitch the pairs into halves. Press seam open.

And finally, stitch the halves into a whole star. Press seams open.

The star should measure 6½" unfinished.

New York Beauty Blocks – Make 16

Make a template for the Pie, Solid Arc, and Background shapes (templates on page 86). Don't forget the 16 Spire Arcs called for under Foundations You Will Use.

Cut out 16 Pie and Background shapes following the directions on pages 11–12.

Making sure that the green fabric is heavily starched for this step, cut out 16 of the Solid Arc shapes, leaving approximately ¼" (for good piecers) to ½" extra (for not so good piecers) on the straight edge ONLY. The curves are cut to the curve.

Stitch the Solid Arc to the Pie with the Pie shape on top. Press toward the Arc. Stitch the Spire Arc to this unit with the Spire Arc on top. Press toward the Spire Arc. Add the Background, stitching with the Background piece on top. Press toward the Background.

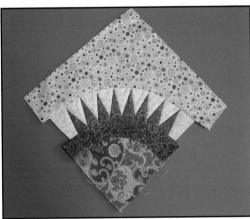

Ruler Placement for Final Trim

Place the 1½" line in the seam allowance between the Background and the Spire Arc.

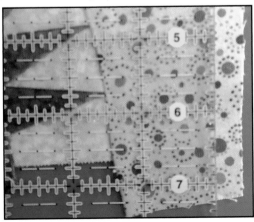

The diagonal line of the ruler will go through the center of the Spires in the Arc.

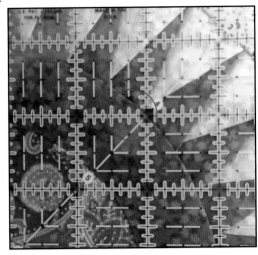

After double checking to make sure you have at least ¼" from the bottom of the last Spire to the 6½" line on the ruler (so you have a ¼"seam allowance), make your first trimming cut. Turn the block and trim to 6½" (no special ruler placement required).

LITTLE RED ROCHESTER, 34½" x 34½",
made by Rebecca Szabo, Howell, New Jersey.
Quilted by the author.

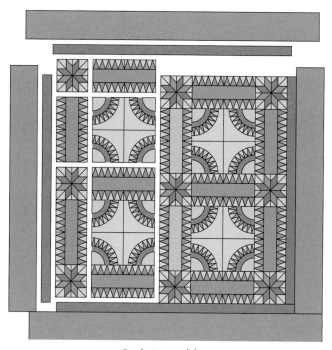

Quilt Assembly

Quilting Design

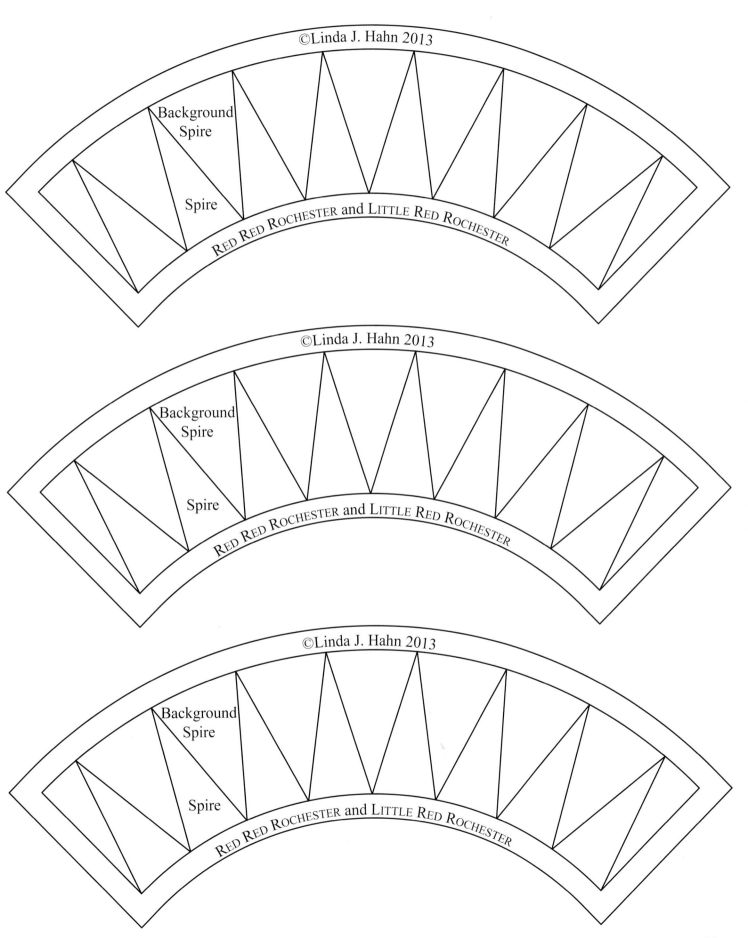

©Linda J. Hahn 2013

Background
Spire

Spire

RED RED ROCHESTER and LITTLE RED ROCHESTER

©Linda J. Hahn 2013

Background
Spire

Spire

RED RED ROCHESTER and LITTLE RED ROCHESTER

©Linda J. Hahn 2013

Background
Spire

Spire

RED RED ROCHESTER and LITTLE RED ROCHESTER

©Linda J. Hahn 2013

Background
Spire

Spire

Red Red Rochester and Little Red Rochester

Red Red Rochester and Little Red Rochester
Background

Red Red Rochester and Little Red Rochester
Solid Arc

Red Red Rochester and
Little Red Rochester

Pie

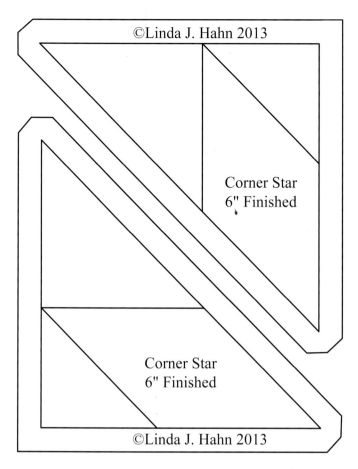

Corner Star
6" Finished

Corner Star
6" Finished

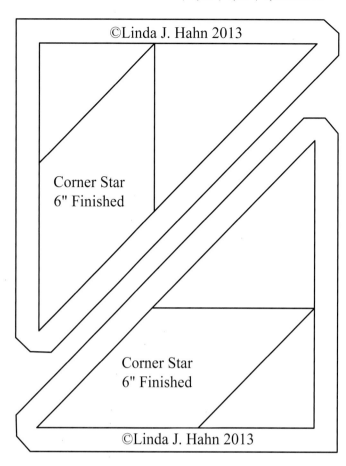

Corner Star
6" Finished

Corner Star
6" Finished

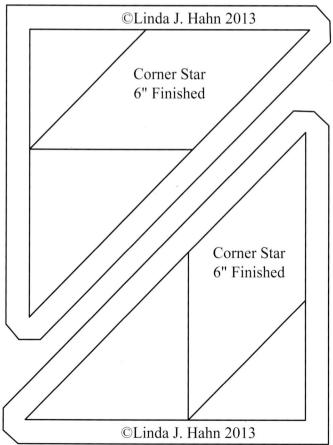

Corner Star
6" Finished

Corner Star
6" Finished

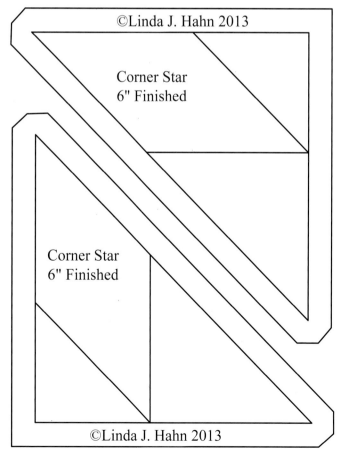

Corner Star
6" Finished

Corner Star
6" Finished

Hues of the Hudson, 47" x 47". Designed, made and quilted by Sarah L. Hahn, Manalapan, New Jersey.

Hues of the

HUDSON

This quilt show how you can incorporate the mix and match blocks into a medallion-style quilt. The sample quilts was quilted using the Fascination pantograph pattern.

Blocks or Units You Will Make
- 28 New York Beauty blocks with Regular Arcs (page 11)
- 4 New York Beauty blocks with Split Spire Arcs (page 11)
- 8 Spire Strips (page 11)
- 28 Simple Square-in-a-Square blocks (page 68)
- Four 16-Patch blocks (page 89)

Foundations Methods You Will Use
- 28 Regular Arcs (template on page 93). Use EQ paper. 2 per page = 14 pages.
- 14 Split Spire Arcs (template on page 94). Use EQ paper. 1 per page = 14 pages.
- 8 Spire Strips (5-point) (template on page 93). Use EQ paper. 4 per page = 2 pages.
- 28 Simple Square-in-a-Square blocks (4" finished); see page 68.

Fabrics
- **Red print:**
    Cut 28 squares 4½" x 4½" (Pies)
    Cut 12 rectangles 1½" x 3½" (Background Spires)
    Cut 16 strips 1½" by width of fabric (16-Patches)

- **Pink/orange print:** ½ yard
    Cut 12 rectangles 1½" x 3½" (Split Spires)
    Cut 28 squares 4½" x 4½"
        (Square-in-a-Square blocks)

- **Dark blue:** ¼ yard (Backgrounds)
    Cut 4 squares 8" x 8"

- **Dark blue print:**
    Cut 12 rectangles 1½" x 3½" (Spires)
    Cut 140 rectangles 2½" x 3½" (Spires)
    Cut 28 rectangles 3" x 3½" (Spire Strips)
    Cut 16 strips 1½" by width of fabric (16-Patches)

- **Medium blue print:** ⅜ yard
    Cut 4 squares 4½" x 4½" (Pies)
    Cut 32 squares 2½" x 2½"
        (Square-in-a-Square blocks)

- **Light teal:** 1⅓ yards (Background Spires)
    Cut 168 rectangles 3" x 4"

- **Dark teal print:** ½ yard
    Cut 224 squares 8" x 8" (Backgrounds)
    Cut 24 rectangles 3" x 3½" (Spire Strips)

- **Dark purple print:** ¾ yard
    Cut 2 squares 9½" x 9½" in half on the diagonal (Center Triangles)
    Cut 2 squares 3" x 3" in half on the diagonal (Corner Spire Strip)
    Cut 5 strips 2½" x width of fabric (Binding)

- **Backing and matching hanging sleeve:** 3¼ yards
    2 cuts 40" x 55" each, pieced vertically

- **Batting:** 55" x 55"

- **Binding:** ½ yard included in Dark purple print yardage

Sewing
Make:
- 28 New York Beauty blocks with Regular Arcs
- 4 New York Beauty blocks with Split Spires
- 8 Spire Strips
- 28 Square-in-a-Square blocks (use the method on page 68)
- 4 (four) 16-Patch blocks
- 5 strip-sets alternating 2 strips of red and 2 strips of dark blue:
        Blue
        Red
        Blue
        Red
- 5 strip-sets of:
        Red
        Blue
        Red
        Blue

Cross cut each strip-set into 1½" segments to total 56 of each. Alternating the colors, stitch 4 strip-sets together. Repeat to create 28 four-row 16-Patch units.

Assembly

To assemble this quilt, start in the center and work outwards.

1) Stitch 4 of the Split Spire blocks together into a Full Sun.

2) Stitch 2 Spire Strips together along the short side. Repeat to make 3 additional Spire Strips.

3) Stitch 1 Spire Strip each on the left and right sides of the Full Sun block.

4) Add 1 purple triangle to each end of the remaining 2 Spire Strips.

5) Add 1 of these Split Spire units each to the top and the bottom of the Full Sun block.

6) Stitch 1 large purple triangle to each corner. Trim the completed center to 19½" x 19½".

7) Alternating the orientation of the 16-Patch blocks AND their placement, stitch them to the Square-in-a-Square blocks. Your goal is to create 4 pieced strips to surround the center block. Add these strips to the sides first, then the top and bottom.

8) Following the diagram of the quilt, stitch together 2 sets of 6 Regular Arc New York Beauty blocks. Add 1 to each side of the quilt top. Stitch together 2 sets of 8 Regular Arc New York Beauty blocks. Add these sets to the top and the bottom of the quilt top.

Quilt, bind, label, and admire!

Quilt Assembly

Quilting Design

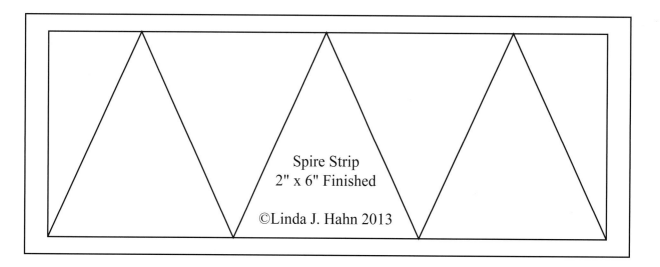

Spire Strip
2" x 6" Finished

©Linda J. Hahn 2013

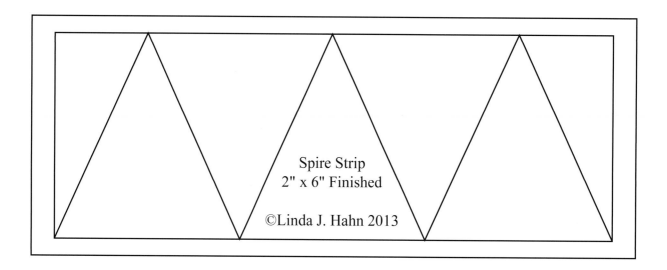

Spire Strip
2" x 6" Finished

©Linda J. Hahn 2013

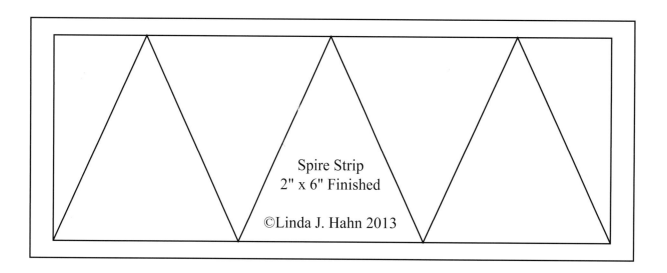

Spire Strip
2" x 6" Finished

©Linda J. Hahn 2013

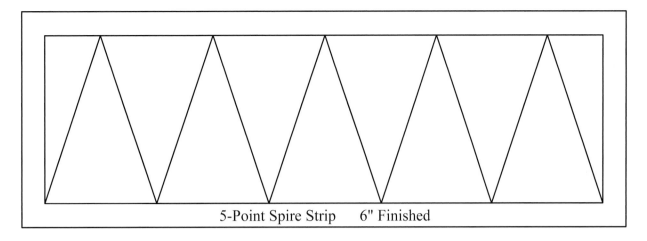

5-Point Spire Strip   6" Finished

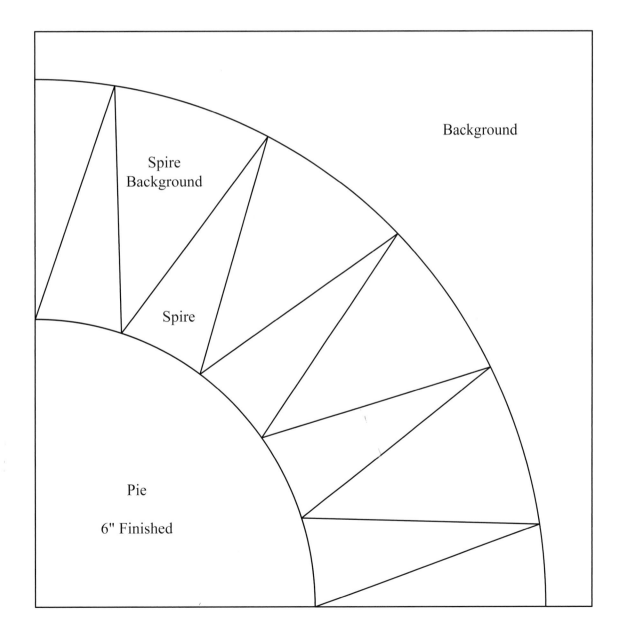

Background

Spire
Background

Spire

Pie

6" Finished

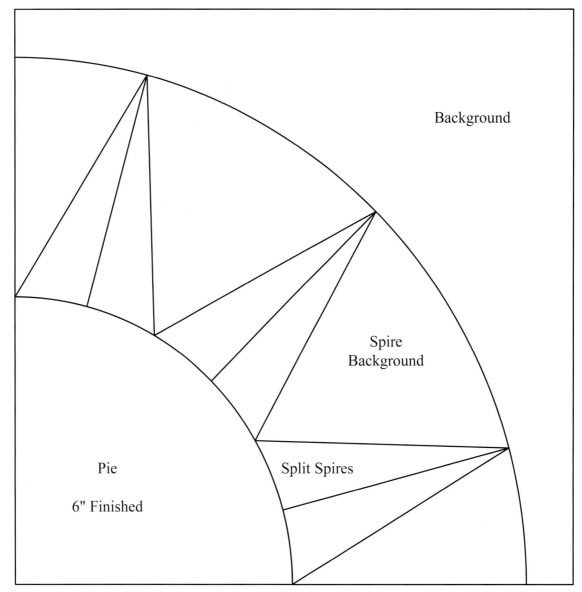

Background

Spire
Background

Pie

6" Finished

Split Spires

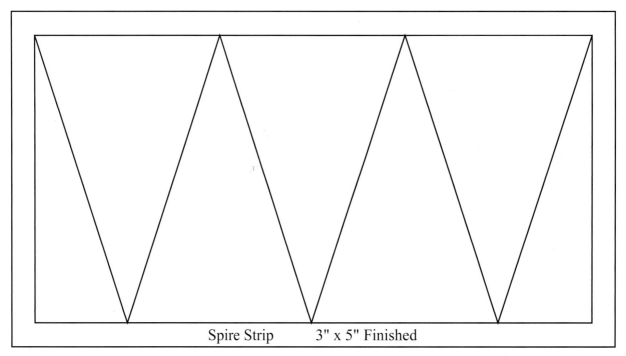

Spire Strip   3" x 5" Finished

Resources

Acrylic Template Sets, Foundation Paper, Paper Piecing & Quilting Stencils, Kits - all your New York Beauty supplies!

Frog Hollow Designs, www.froghollowdesigns.com

Machine Quilting Services for Your New York Beauty Quilts

Sarah L. Hahn, sarah@froghollowdesigns.com

Fabrics

Hoffman California Fabrics, www.hoffmanfabrics.com

Northcott Silk, Inc., www.northcott.com

Timeless Treasures, www.ttfabrics.com

Clothworks, Inc., www.clothworks.com

Elizabeth's Studio, LLC, www.elizabethsstudio.word-press.com

Quilt Shops

Quilting Possibilities. www.quiltingposs.com

Olde City Quilts, www.oldecityquilts.com

Foundation Paper

The Electric Quilt Company, www.electricquilt.com

Rulers and Notions

Prym Consumer USA, www.prym-consumer-usa.com

Threads

Superior Threads, www.superiorthreads.com

Sulky of America, www.sulky.com

New York Beauty Paper Piecing Stencils and Quilting Stencils

Quilting Creations International, www.quiltingcreations.com

Batting/Fusible

The Warm Company, www.warmcompany.com

Quilter's Dream Batting, www.quiltersdreambatting.com

Starch

Magic Sizing, www.faultless.com

Reference Books

Bobbin Quiltin' and Fusin' Fun by Michele Scott (AQS, 2011)

Free Motion Quilting by Judy Woodworth (AQS, 2010)

About the Author

When she was introduced to quilting in 1993, Linda Hahn couldn't even thread a sewing machine. She retired from her job as a paralegal in 2005 to begin working in the quilt industry full time.

Linda loves to teach quilting. She was the 2009 NQA Certified Teacher of the Year. She has been nominated three times for Professional Quilter Magazine's Teacher of the Year award. Her specialty is taking complex-looking blocks and breaking them down into understandable, easy steps so that everyone can enjoy them.

In addition to being an author and teacher, Linda also is a longarm quilter, a pattern designer, and a magazine contributor. Her patterns are marketed as Frog Hollow Designs (www.froghollowdesigns.com). Her first book was *New York Beauty Simplified* (AQS, 2010).

Linda lives in Manalapan, New Jersey, with her husband Allan, daughter Sarah, and rescue Golden Retriever Amber. Sarah quilted most of the quilts in this book. When Linda is not quilting or visiting guilds to encourage a "New York Beauty state of mind," she can be found on a cruise ship somewhere in the sunny Caribbean.

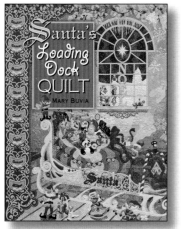
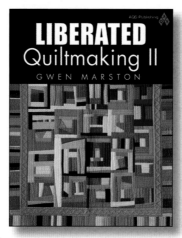
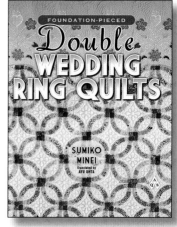

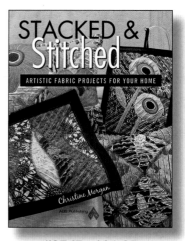

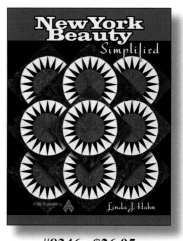